# CAPITAL
# WALKS

## WALKING TOURS OF OTTAWA

## KATHARINE FLETCHER

M&S

**Canadian Cataloguing in Publication Data**

Fletcher, Katharine, 1952–
   Capital walks :   walking tours of Ottawa

ISBN 0–7710–3151–3

1.  Historic buildings  –  Ontario  –  Ottawa  –  Guidebooks.
2.   Architecture  –  Ontario  –  Ottawa  –  Guidebooks.   3. Ottawa (Ont.)
–  Buildings, sculptures, etc.  –  Guidebooks.   4. Ottawa (Ont.)  –  Tours.
I.   Title.

FC3096.18.F57  1993          917.13′84044          C93–093190–4
F1059.5.09F57  1993


The publishers acknowledge the support of the Canada Council and the Ontario Arts Council for their publishing program.

Printed and bound in Canada. The paper used in this book is acid-free.

McClelland & Stewart Inc.
*The Canadian Publishers*
481 University Avenue
Toronto, Ontario
M5G 2E9

We learn much from those who go before us. *Capital Walks* is dedicated to the memory of Michael Newton, a heritage friend.

# Contents

# Preface

It is a shame that few residents or visitors go off the beaten track to explore Ottawa's back lanes, cobbled courtyards and many splendid vistas. There are stories of men and women, clues to the capital's historic past, among its neighbourhood streets and in its buildings. This is why I decided to write *Capital Walks*: because there is much to treasure here in the cozy communities and grand boulevards that set the tone and mood of Ottawa.

Ottawa is blessed with heritage buildings, both modern and historical. Among these pages you will find the Commissariat, the oldest stone building in Ottawa, built by Thomas MacKay's Scottish stonemasons in 1827, beside the Rideau Canal. While standing in front of it you can look up and decide for yourself how well architects Rysavy & Rysavy have integrated their 1992 Canadian Museum of Contemporary Photography with its next-door neighbour, the 1908–12 Chateau Laurier.

Our built environment is a constantly evolving organism, with a dynamic life of its own. Ottawa is no exception. In the three years it took me to research and write *Capital Walks*, some buildings have been torn down, others altered, and infill added. And certain demolitions of years ago still linger in my mind as regrettable losses to the capital's streetscape. One such "old friend" was the 1854 Clegg house at 154 Bay. I remember this house's passing: for months it stood exposed, half torn asunder, while the City battled with its owners, the trustees of St. Peter's Evangelical Lutheran Church. They have the unfortunate distinction of being the first owners to be prosecuted under the Ontario Heritage Act in 1979. Today there is a parking lot where the house once stood. Too many other heritage buildings, like the technically innovative Aberdeen Pavilion, are under constant threat of demolition.

But change is by no means always negative. Ottawans today enjoy the beautiful parklands and bicycle paths bordering the Ottawa River. Yet the historic mills of New Edinburgh that once hummed to the power of the Rideau Falls first had to be torn down. Gone, too, is the bustling industrial and residential community of Lowertown North, victim to "urban planning" and "relocation." These words give scant comfort to the people who lost their homes. But for those of us who follow, the grassy parkland that replaced them soothes the eye and lifts the spirit.

I love this city. In 1974, during my final year at Trent University, in Peterborough, I faced the question every graduate faces: where to go to build a future and carve a niche for myself. I had fond memories of the capital city after a grade ten school trip introduced me to Gatineau Park and the sights of Ottawa. My first book, *Historical Walks: The Gatineau Park Story*, was really born then, when as a young schoolgirl I climbed King Mountain and surveyed the Ottawa River, the route of Champlain's grand adventure in 1613. In 1974 I made my decision. I moved to Ottawa and learned its streets and ways by bicycle, bus, canoe, skates – and on foot. It's that kind of a city: its many paths, waterways and streets invite exploration and beckon, no matter the season.

Now I live in an old farmhouse near Quyon, in West Quebec. Since 1989 I have lived beside my beloved Gatineau Park, and I am a resident of the National Capital Region created by the vision of Jacques Gréber in his Master Plan of 1951. But Ottawa is still a part of me. Today, I visit the city perhaps twice a week, and I have gained a different perspective now that I am a visitor. I get a surprise – sometimes a jolt – as a streetscape suddenly shifts its mood with the addition of another architect's or planner's vision. Although I dearly cherish the past, I also enjoy the city's evolution.

I hope that *Capital Walks* will help you to get to know Ottawa. Take the time to saunter, to browse and to savour the city's neighbourhoods. Carry a backpack and a lunch – or try a new restaurant. Above all, have fun getting to know the city's special places. And, if you want to read more about Ottawa's history and heritage buildings, refer to my "Further Reading" section at the back of the book.

# A Question of Style

If they were asked to identify their city's most significant building, most Ottawans would point to the spires of Parliament Hill, the symbolic centre of the nation. But the restored façade of stone and brick buildings which crowd Sussex Drive and lead the eye down to Notre-Dame's twin steeples and the National Gallery equally well define the capital. And just as representative of the city as these public and commercial edifices are the houses in which Ottawans, past and present, live. A walk along the tree-lined avenues of Ottawa's first suburb, the Glebe, shows us the city's typical two- and three-storey red brick houses, many with gambrel roofs, others with front end-gables facing the street. Lowertown's busy streets lend the city a distinctly French-Canadian flavour. Here, dormers project from steeply pitched roofs, carriageways lead to rear courtyards and "cliffhanger," second-storey porches distinguish its streetscape.

Structures have their own form, function and *raison d'être*. What influences the choice of style varies from building to building. Sometimes it is the whim of a politician, such as former prime ministers Mackenzie King, who liked the châteauesque style, and Pierre Elliott Trudeau, who chose architect Moshe Safdie's "extrovert" not his "introvert" design for the National Gallery. Often style is dictated by a detail as perfunctory as budget. Sometimes Nature deals the architect a wild card, like an unstable leda clay foundation. And sometimes a new technology allows stylistic experimentation or an owner insists on a period style. What is certain is that every building is the product of design constraints and the imagination of the architect, builder and owner.

The style of neighborhoods also varies, because of zoning restrictions, the wealth of its residents, the era in which it was built. Each Ottawa neighbourhood possesses a unique atmosphere and charm. Rockcliffe Village's large lots and mansions are not comparable to the congested lots of New Edinburgh, originally designed by Thomas MacKay as a millworkers' village. Yet the two complement each other. Together, the neighbourhoods of Ottawa form a tapestry of textures, colour and design – a livable city.

## The Early Days

*The Kingston Chronicle* of March 9, 1827, announced: "We rejoice to hear that it is resolved to build a town to be named after Lieutenant Colonel By of the Royal Engineers." It is fitting that Ottawa was first named for a man of military background, for Bytown's *raison d'être* was strategic defence after the War of 1812. What Britain wanted was an inland line of communications, so that militia supplies and men could be transported along a defensible corridor. As Chief Engineer, By was responsible for the construction of the 200-kilometre Rideau Canal that extends from Entrance Bay on the Ottawa River to Kingston. As soon as the canal project was discussed, Bytown experienced an infusion of capital and residents as land speculators and labourers joined the already-booming lumber and service community.

Ottawa's first buildings were log shanties, constructed from immediately available local timber, which provided homesteaders with rudimentary shelter. As the walls went up, spaces between the logs were carefully chinked with clay or moss. Roofs of wooden shingles or strips of bark were common. Windows – if cut at all— were covered with oiled paper until glass panes could be afforded. When windows were cut, they were usually small, for the winters were long and bitterly cold. Floors were first of bare earth and, later, the dirt was

*Earliest shelters were crude log structures.* W. H. Bartlett print, NCC 172

covered with wooden planks. Limestone slabs packed with clay fashioned the fireplace, and a hole in the roof served as a chimney.

These first dwellings were replaced by houses of brick and stone as soon as the homesteaders could afford it. Thomas MacKay's Scottish stonemasons, who built the Rideau Canal, found ready employment building this "second wave" of dwellings and public edifices. Today, the capital still boasts many examples of their masonry skills. Classical features such as regularly spaced windows with a central doorway typify these early permanent structures. The Commissariat (1827), the Fraser Schoolhouse (1837) and the Donnelly House (1844) exhibit the solidity and simplicity of this design. But, before stone could become a common building material, an infrastructure of construction apparatus, transportation routes, money and skilled craftsmen were required. After the opening of the railways, such as the Bytown and Prescott in 1854, materials could be brought in from remote and even exotic locations. By Confederation in 1867, most ordinary people's houses were of frame construction, although most commercial buildings were brick or stone.

The *Ottawa City Directory* of 1866 details the wealth of material that was available to local builders: "Beside the Arnprior marble, the district of Ottawa furnishes all kinds of building stone. A black or grey limestone which gives a fine massive appearance to buildings, and which has been extensively used in this neighbourhood, is known as the Trenton limestone. A very beautiful white or light-yellow freestone is found at Nepean; and another, white as Carrara marble, is found at Perth."

By 1866, the spires of Parliament graced the Hill. The East and West blocks, designed by architects Stent and Laver, and Thomas Fuller's original Centre Block (which burned in 1916) and Parliamentary Library, were all built between 1859 and 1865. The architects incorporated local stone into their design as it made aesthetic and economic sense. Their picturesque Gothic Revival designs inspired contemporary architects and builders to use local materials with confidence and pride. Local industries reaped the benefit as quarries, sandpits, brickworks, foundries, lumber mills and skilled craftsmen met the requirements of the capital's swelling population and housing needs.

Thomas Coltrin Keefer's 1864 map of Rockcliffe clearly shows a deposit of white marl. Thomas Clark recognized an opportunity here, and by 1872 his brickworks were producing the red and white brick that was used extensively in the capital region. Entrepreneurial opportunity presents itself in different ways to different people: Thomas Woodburn, carpenter at MacKay's New Edinburgh mills, built his Victorian Gothic double (73–73 MacKay Street) in 1874. Its fanciful wishbone-shaped gingerbread trim, called bargeboard, and pretty wooden porches were an effective advertisement of his trade and skill. Woodburn's ornate carpentry work was possible because of the coincidence of several factors: the ready availability of wood, such comparatively new technical advances as the jig saw, and his proximity to the New Edinburgh mills.

By the late 1800s, the enduring Gothic Revival style, with its picturesque ornamentation of steeply gabled roofs, pointed arch windows, lacy bargeboard (gingerbread), bay and oriel windows became re-interpreted in a variety of ways. The Queen Anne style was the most whimsical extension of Gothic and was especially popular for houses. A major characteristic was asymmetrical massing, which held special appeal after the more rigid lines of classical design. Houses now featured picturesque external silhouettes which, on the interior, translated into a flexible floor plan. Number 500 Wilbrod, the Fleck House, and, in a more rare example of commercial architecture, the Central Chambers on Elgin reflect the late Victorian love of colour, mixed texture and form as interpreted in the Queen Anne style.

But other styles and influences competed in the neighbourhoods of Ottawa. In 1905, three hundred master stonemasons and stone-cutters from Scotland built architect David Ewart's castle-like Victoria Memorial Museum, today known as the Museum of Nature. Like the Scottish masons brought here in the 1820s by Thomas MacKay for the construction of the Rideau Canal, Ewart's stonemasons settled in the Ottawa area, and went on to build many private houses and public buildings. Ewart's triptych on Sussex Drive, the Connaught Building, the War Museum and the Mint, all are monumental edifices that further utilized skills of these stonemasons.

## New Technologies

But the construction of multiple-storied, multiple-windowed office towers – what became generally known as *skyscrapers* in the 1880s – had to wait supporting technologies. Although the term had been used by the 1840s to describe buildings of four storeys (in addition to tall tales and tall people) it was popularized after the 1885 construction of a completely steel frame insurance building in Chicago, designed by architect Louis Sullivan.

The 1890 Central Chambers on Elgin Street is Ottawa's first experiment with vertical bay windows. This innovative fenestration, which today seems technically unremarkable, although beautiful, was possible only because architect John James Browne used the new technology of steel girders to build a sturdy frame. However, the weight of his building is still supported on masonry load-bearing walls: its steel girders rest upon brick structural walls.

The Central Chambers was also one of the first buildings in the capital to incorporate electric elevators. Reliable elevators meant people could be transported up and down multi-floored buildings. Technologies such as electricity, and new systems for indoor plumbing and ventilation coincided with inventions such as the telephone, and modern skyscrapers were born.

As the 1900s advanced, steel cage construction with stone exterior sheathing was increasingly used for commercial buildings. Architect W. E. Noffke (1878–1964) designed the Blackburn Building at 85 Sparks with fire resistance clearly in mind: its steel frame is covered by a non-structural façade of concrete and brick. On the southeast corner of Rideau and Sussex stands the Transportation Building (1916), designed by architect N. Ogilvie. This building exhibits its steel skeleton frame construction, with repetitive bands of windows topped by an exposed, elaborate copper cornice. It is a good example of how the change in technology liberated earlier height restrictions. Stone walls couldn't support multi-storeys simply because of their own weight, whereas steel frames could. They truly birthed the skyscraper phenomenon.

In the early years of the twentieth century, many architects reached back into historical memory, and designed structures inspired by Second Empire, Italianate, Scottish baronial and Romanesque Revival traditions. For example, the Second Empire Langevin Block on the corner of Elgin and Wellington sports a deep mansard roof. The mansard roofline (named after seventeenth century French architect François Mansart) permitted the use of the attic floor as functional, and well-insulated space. The incorporation of dormer or Palladian windows set into the mansard's lines allows light into the top floor. In the Langevin Block the mansard roof is highly ornamented and grand; a simpler version of the mansard was a popular roof design for private houses. You will discover it in every Ottawa neighbourhood – and all construction periods. Many of today's post-modern buildings, such as the mall on Beechwood (*see* New Edinburgh walk), have mansard roofs.

W. E. Noffke was inspired with the sheer walls and clean lines of the Spanish Colonial Revival style. Perhaps his best building is at 85 Glebe Avenue, overlooking Central Park. Designed as part of a planned community development by the Clemow-Powell realty firm, this house is one of several that Noffke created bordering the park. Noffke was a prodigious producer of more than 200 Ottawa buildings which widely varied in style. His Spanish Colonial residences, although in a revivalist style, still impart a freshness to the streetscape. Those such as 85 Glebe seem far closer in feeling to the modernist movement of pared-down and organic design, than the asymmetrical massing and picturesque silhouettes of Victorian Gothic and Queen Anne.

Architect Francis Sullivan (1882–1929) was inspired by architect Frank Lloyd Wright and his Prairie School philosophy. Wright became his friend and mentor. Wright spurned historical motifs and promoted the concept of organic, environmental design. Sullivan's 1914 Horticultural Building at Lansdowne Park displays the horizontal planes and wide overhanging eaves typical of Prairie School design. Noffke occasionally incorporates the *feeling* of Prairie Style into such homes as the Glebe's 517 O'Connor (1913). Here he uses the extension of a covered carriageway or *porte-cochère* on one side and a balancing covered sunroom on the other to achieve a sense of horizontality.

And then the war of 1914–18 came, destroying a way of life and vision of the world. After the Depression years of the 1930s and World War II, architects wanted to move ahead, not to look backwards for inspiration. An enthusiasm to experiment with forms, coupled with the prohibitively expensive cost in materials and labour associated with the ornate revivalist styles, stimulated the new, minimalist designs of the modern movement.

One experimentation with space and form grew into the recognizable styles of modernism also known as the International Style. The movement was born in Europe in the 1920s at the Bauhaus school in Germany. Architects such as Mies van der Rohe and Walter Gropius were leaders of the modern movement who were tremendously influential internationally after they fled Germany during Hitler's regime to England and the United States. Internationalist buildings celebrate the technological advances of cantilevered construction, and concrete, glass and steel replace wood, brick and stone as the primary materials. External ornamentation is reviled, and repetition encouraged. The many storeys resemble one another: one band of horizontal ribbon windows is placed upon another, emphasizing rather than obscuring the steel skeleton-frame construction.

Modernism in Ottawa is represented in such buildings as the old International Style city hall (1958) on Green Island and two residences in Sandy Hill (265 Goulburn and 68 Range). In Rockcliffe Village, Hart Massey's International Style design for his own home at 400 Lansdowne Road won him a Massey Award in 1959. This residence is a "cubist" delight, a composition of exposed steel frames with a glassed front overlooking MacKay Lake and, on the street façade, inset wood panels for privacy. However, modernism, typified by its "factory-like" appearance of sheer, flat walls and rectilinear planes was never popular with the public, especially not for private houses. Most people in the post-war years opted for comforting period revival styles or else the convenient new bungalow house, with its cozy spaces and broad, welcoming porches.

Ottawa's built environment continues to reflect changing styles and new technologies. The Ottawa Courthouse on Elgin is a recent example of Brutalism, a style which evolved in the 1960s and 1970s and which became popular on university campuses such as the University of Ottawa. The Court's monumental, sheer walls are unrelieved save by narrow, almost inconsequential strips of windows. The humanizing touches in this imposing court are experienced only in its interior spaces, which are flooded with natural light from a triangular-shaped atrium. On the street, the courthouse is delightfully offset by the heritage Teacher's College of rough-faced limestone. Built on a human scale, this 1874 composition is as welcoming as its neighbour is intimidating.

Post-modern office buildings now dot the Ottawa landscape. Post-modernist style is an intriguing "new look backwards" which features the attempt to integrate historical ornamentation and idiosyncratic detail into concrete and glass structures. Such motifs as stylized mansard or steeply pitched roofs and dormer windows have been incorporated into new structures such as the small mall on Beechwood, directly opposite Alistair Ross's post-modern Royal Bank at 25 Beechwood. Similarly, Barrister House on Elgin opposite the old Teacher's College is a highrise post-modern tower.

## Fire

External influences directly affect the construction and style of a building. One such factor is fire, which repeatedly ravaged the twin cities of Ottawa and Hull. Both lighting and heating were provided

*Fleeing the 1900 fire.* NCC, M. Newton Heritage file E12-0-11; Box 39

by open flame in the first wooden and stone buildings. Whale oil and then gas illuminated all buildings, from the lowliest cottages to the vice-regal residence, Rideau Hall. Open hearths, wood-burning stoves and the furnaces of the early forges, mills and tanneries contributed to the threat of fire. Until the late 1800s the all-too-frequent fires were extremely difficult to extinguish because water had to be drawn laboriously by horse and cart to the site in large barrels called puncheons. Some puncheon drivers haggled with owners over the fee – while houses and businesses perished in flames. In the Great Fire of 1900, flames leapt across the river from Hull, turning the piled lumber stored on Victoria Island into infernos. The fire almost destroyed Ottawa – only a shift in wind direction saved the capital.

Fire prevention was thus a major consideration for architects and builders throughout the early years. On February 3, 1916, fire swept through the Centre Block of Parliament. The only surviving part of Thomas Fuller's original design is the Library. Fuller had incorporated a steel fire door into his design that isolated the Library from the flames.

## The Shape of Ottawa

Topography and layout also influence the design and shape of a city. The men who surveyed Ottawa were British, and they used a regular-spaced grid layout for property and street definition. Ottawa is further described by lot sizes that characterize individual neighbourhoods. For example, Lowertown's houses, built on tiny lots, bear little resemblance to those on nearby Metcalfe Street, where grand old mansions give a hint of that street's early ambitions to be a ceremonial approach to Parliament Hill.

The 1919 community of Lindenlea represents a planned garden homes suburb. Based upon English architect Thomas Adams' popular concept for suburban living, Lindenlea is not on a grid pattern: its streets curve and flow into one another, forming yet another shape inside the city.

The balance between lot and building size is a key design element, and the most attractive buildings are scaled to their environment. New Edinburgh's 34 Alexander is a whimsical Second Empire home that sports flamboyant wishbone gables. Once renowned for its splendid gardens, today it is a victim of additions, and it perches forlornly in its now tiny grounds. In contrast, the horizontal planes of

*A typical Glebe street with red brick homes and enclosed porches. Oct. 1991.* K. Fletcher

the Danish Embassy in Rockcliffe Village nestle agreeably into its hillside in a truly organic design.

Far different are the tightly packed streetscapes of St. Patrick Street in Lowertown. The Irish and French workers who first lived here never enjoyed large, treed gardens. Instead, their backyards contained only cramped outhouse toilets and perhaps a stable. In the years 1850–70, Lowertown, and especially the Byward Market, was the commercial centre of Ottawa. Successive waves of immigrants chose it as their new home. On tiny lots they constructed small buildings that were both their business and residence. Those that could afford to build a double did so, and rented them for income. The flavour of Lowertown's neighbourhood became peppered with European accents, with trades such as saddle, shoe, carriage and candle makers beside colourful market stalls.

Today, space is increasingly at a premium throughout the city, in every neighbourhood. Lots are rezoned to permit the construction of infill houses or additions, and architects now win prizes for infill projects. As well, highrise apartment buildings and condominiums

*View southeast from the Peace Tower, around 1890; foreground: East Block; left: canal with Major's Hill with Chapel of Ease (burned 1912) on east side of Sussex St. facing George; right rear shows Canal Basin. NCC 172*

*View north along the Rideau Canal in 1961. Note the railway tracks east of the canal.* NCC 172-22

have forever altered the profile of the streetscape. The character of a neighbourhood perceptibly changes when the density of families, pets, businesses and traffic increases. Rockcliffe Village is no stranger to this. In 1992 Thomas MacKay's 1865 Victorian stone "cottage," Birkenfels, was razed. Today its spacious grounds are broken up into small estate lots and at least one house, 272 Soper Place, has been built in a scale too large for its gentle wooded setting.

The debate over the intrinsic value of open space is ongoing. In 1992, a wrecker's bulldozer demolished the last remains of Moses C. Edey's 1905 landmark, the Daly building. As soon as its walls came down, light and space illuminated the northwest corner of Rideau and Sussex. It exposed hitherto unseen views of David Ewart's massive, castle-like Connaught Building, the Chateau Laurier, and the restored façade of Sussex Drive. The National Capital Commission consider the space too valuable to be left as an open park. But the people of Ottawa still lobby for the preservation of this liberating open area.

## A Capital Mood

Ottawa's style has been studied relentlessly since Queen Victoria decided, in 1857, to locate Canada's capital here. At that time, city founders, architects and residents alike looked about them at the

*The Chateau Laurier Hotel from the roof terrace of the Rideau Centre, 1991.* K. Fletcher

small town surrounding Colonel By's military barracks and wondered if their homes, businesses and public buildings were fit to grace the new capital. They unanimously agreed that what they saw did not quite measure up. The congregation of the first Christ Church Cathedral built in 1832 decided their building was unsuited to Ottawa's new capital status. They hired architect King Arnoldi to design a new church and requested he keep the cost of the project below $25,000. (Arnoldi demurred: he submitted a bill of just less than $50,000.)

The intervening years have seen much torn down, much changed in order to satisfy what succeeding generations of architects, consultants, prime ministers and developers have deemed to be structures befitting the capital of an emerging nation.

Sir Wilfrid Laurier's Liberal government created the capital's first planning body: the Ottawa Improvement Commission (OIC) in 1899. This was the first of three commissions mandated with the task of beautifying Ottawa.

Operating on an annual budget of $60,000, the four commissioners of the OIC made sweeping recommendations that resulted in large-scale improvements to Ottawa. To their credit goes the clean-up of the industrial sprawl of warehouses and construction materials along the canal, where Union Station now stands. Under the leadership of Montreal landscape architect Frederick G. Todd, the OIC was especially successful in the construction of parkways, drives and public squares. Patterson Creek was defined, the Queen Elizabeth Driveway was started, and responsibility for the maintenance of Rockcliffe Park was transferred to the federal government.

In 1913, Sir Robert Borden appointed the Sir Henry Holt Commission which two years later released a report, the first to identify the need for a national capital region beyond the borders of the city. It also recommended the relocation of railway lines away from the downtown core. But World War I and the devastating loss of the Centre Block to fire drained the coffers of government. Holt's recommendations were shelved.

The Federal District Commission (FDC) was appointed in 1927. It was given an annual budget of $250,000, and under its control Ottawa was transformed. Prime Minister Mackenzie King took personal interest in the FDC and championed land acquisition for the creation of a ceremonial grand boulevard to Parliament Hill. His proposal was accepted and a special budget of $3 million was passed. Confederation Square is part of King's, and the FDC's, legacy to Ottawa.

King met Parisian urban planner Jacques Gréber in Paris in 1937 and invited him to Ottawa. They spent long hours discussing the ceremonial approach to Parliament. Although basically of like mind, they did not agree on the placement of the War Memorial. Gréber lost. In 1939 King George VI unveiled the War Memorial at the top of Elgin. King later said that Gréber had probably been right, for the memorial disturbs smooth traffic circulation. Later that year the FDC's plans were put on hold when war was declared.

On August 22, 1945, only eight days after armistice, King sent Gréber a letter inviting him back to Ottawa to define a Capital Master Plan under the FDC. Gréber accepted and the Gréber Report was tabled in the House of Commons in the 1951 government of Louis St. Laurent. In 1958 the National Capital Commission (NCC) replaced the FDC. This is Ottawa's present commission.

In 1959 the railway was finally relocated to the southeast of the city. This permitted the creation and landscaping of Colonel By Drive, the building of the National Arts Centre and the conversion of Union Station into today's Government Conference Centre. In the late 1950s, the NCC purchased many properties, transforming them into public parks. These include Rideau Falls Park, Vincent Massey Park, the Greenbelt, and the Gatineau Park. Later, in 1972, the NCC bought the former E. B. Eddy industrial property opposite Parliament Hill on the Hull side of the Ottawa River.

Part of the NCC's mandate is heritage preservation. Although it has been sharply criticized for not doing enough to ensure that historic properties are not lost, the NCC can still be credited with preserving the Sussex Drive façade. Their means, however, are not always appreciated. In 1961 the NCC commenced expropriating property bordering Sussex. Today, many merchants claim the NCC's rents are exorbitant. In 1993 the old 1840–70 block of buildings formerly known as the Institut Jeanne d'Arc is vacant, too expensive for the NCC to refurbish and rent in recession-torn Ottawa.

The face of the city is ever-changing. The parking lot on Sussex just north of David Ewart's Connaught Building is the newly designated site of the United States Embassy. At time of printing, the Central Chambers, the Scottish Ontario Chambers and the Bell Canada Block overlooking Confederation Square are all being incorporated into a new office complex. Only change is certain in this capital city.

*Ross and MacFarlane's adaptation of original architect Bradford Lee Gilbert's "Roman bath" classical design for the Grand Trunk Railway's Union Station (1912), today's Government Conference Centre.* PAC-PA-10579

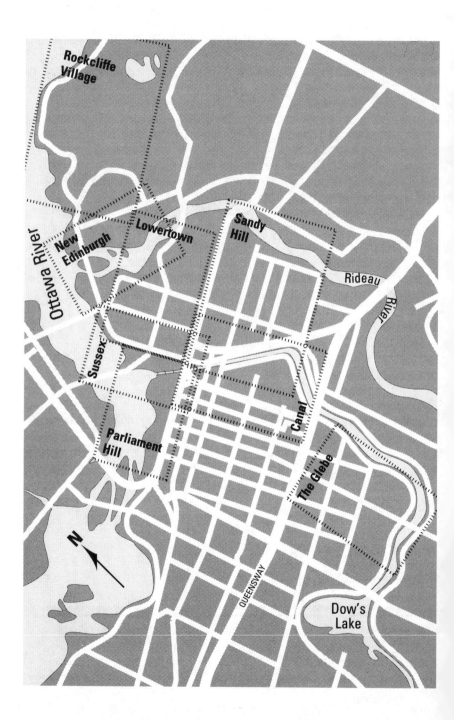

# The Walks

## Walk Tips

The purpose of this book is to introduce you to Ottawa through the exploration of eight neighbourhoods: Parliament Hill, Sussex Drive, Lowertown, New Edinburgh, the Canal, the Glebe, Sandy Hill and Rockcliffe Village. Each walk includes the approximate length in kilometres and an indication of the time to allow.

Here are a few reminders to consider before setting out.

✓ Respect private property: lawns, gardens, and front walks.

✓ Wear comfortable shoes and wear layered clothes so you can take off or put on a sweater or raincoat.

✓ Take along a backpack so you can keep your arms free. The pack can hold your camera, a picnic lunch, binoculars, extra film or a collapsible umbrella.

✓ Take your dog as long as it is restrained on a leash. (And don't forget to stoop and scoop.)

✓ Public washrooms can be found in such buildings as the City Hall, the museums and restaurants. Remember that washrooms in cafés and restaurants are for the use of clientele.

✓ At the time of writing, admission to all museums and to the National Gallery is free on Thursdays. Other days there is a charge and, on Mondays, many galleries and museums are closed. One museum, the Bytown (Commissariat Building, *see* Parliament walk), is closed from late fall through spring.

✓ There are guided tours of the interiors of several public buildings. Most are free, and all tours give you further information on the architect's design and the history of the capital. Watch local newspapers for announcements of special tours such as are given in the height of tourist season.

Finally, explore Ottawa in different seasons and times of the day to enjoy its varied moods. Most of all, have fun discovering the capital.

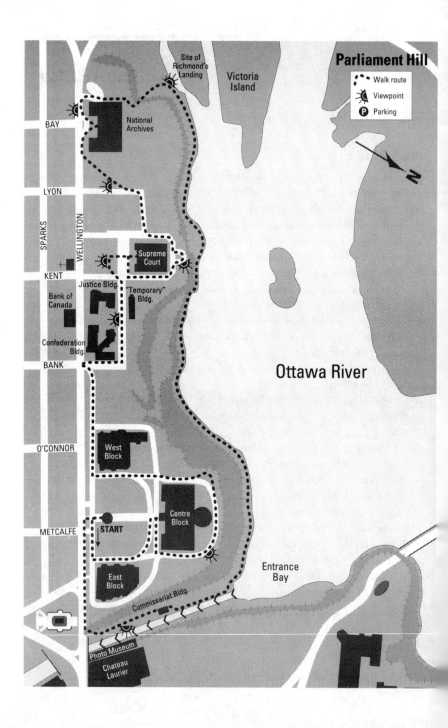

# Parliament Hill

## History

The lofty outcrop of rock overlooking the Ottawa River first determined the city's development. When Lieutenant-Colonel John By, Royal Engineer, arrived in 1826, he agreed with Lord Dalhousie about the site's strategic significance. In 1823 Dalhousie had purchased approximately 400 acres, including what is today's Parliament Hill, for the sum of £750 from settler Hugh Fraser. In 1826 he wrote a letter to By, underscoring the site's suitability for a canal and transferring ownership to By's care. Colonel By then reserved the Hill as a government reserve under Ordnance control and erected a barracks and army hospital. By's principal task was to select a site for the start of the Rideau Canal, which would serve as a military link between the Ottawa River and Kingston. After considering several locations, (including Richmond's Landing, adjacent to LeBreton Flats), By chose

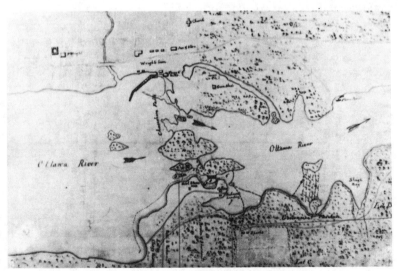

*1825 map of the Ottawa River at Bytown by Major George Eliot. The upper section shows Wrightsville (Hull). PAC-C-16156*

*Wellington Street near Bank, 1853, looking east; watercolour by Lt. C. Sedley. The fence defines government land west of the canal. The rise of land at the rear is Barracks [now Parliament] Hill and the Hospital; homes, businesses and hotels throng either side of Wellington.* PAC-C-1548

the gorge just to the east of the Hill, Entrance Bay, then known as Sleigh Bay. Construction on the canal began in 1826, and in 1832 the 200-kilometre waterway was completed.

When Queen Victoria chose Ottawa as Canada's capital on December 31, 1857, Barracks Hill was deemed the most desirable site for the Parliament Buildings. *The Ottawa Tribune* of May 21, 1859, posted a "Notice to Architects" specifying the budget for the buildings: "For Parliament House, $300,000; for Departmental Bldg. $240,000."

The first sod was turned on December 20, 1859. However, the Centre Block was not completed until six years later. Delays followed one another, and the original budget was quickly exceeded. Problems included instability in the underlying rock bed, the need to install water tanks in case of fire, and the transportation of the stone from the Nepean quarry, twelve miles away. In 1862, a Royal Commission was assigned to study the costly delays that caused layoffs of up to 1,700 skilled tradespeople. The buildings were deemed ready on September 8, 1865, although not all doors and windows had been installed. Still the exterior appearance of Parliament Hill was acclaimed, their Gothic Revival spires described variously as "imposing," "picturesque" and "inspirational."

*Fuller's winning design for Parliament Buildings, Centre Block; lithograph by Burland Lasricain, Montreal. The fountains and stairs represent artistic licence.* NCC 172-116

Unfortunately, the fire precautions were insufficient to prevent flames destroying the Centre Block on February 3, 1916. Only the Library survived the conflagration. Stent and Laver's winning designs for both the East and West blocks were untouched. Canadian poet Duncan Campbell Scott witnessed the spectacle: "The fire was terrible and tragic; it was the most terrifying and beautiful sight I have ever seen. ... I hope that the building may be restored without the practice of any vandalism, but I have my doubts. I hear talk of 'a larger, more imposing, up-to-date building.' The very phrases make one shudder. We had a building that was beautiful and harmonized with the site, and there will be some people who will want to destroy it because they can put up something more beautiful. If they can put up a more beautiful building, let them put it somewhere else. Let us preserve the beauty that we have."[1]

But the structural damage was such that the Centre Block had to be demolished. Architect John A. Pearson's Neo-Gothic design won the ensuing competition and the present Centre Block was erected between 1916 and 1920. During these years the seat of government was located in the Victoria Memorial Museum (now the Museum of Nature; *see* Canal walk) at the foot of Metcalfe Street.

*Construction of Parliament Centre Block (John Pearson, architect) in Nov. 2, 1916. The original Thomas Fuller Library (rear) escaped the fire.* PAC-C-19216

The original workshop that once graced the Hill was demolished to make way for a parking lot in September 1956. This building was located at Bank and Wellington and extended to the entry (now barred) to the Lover's Walk, which descended the cliffs to the river. In its lifetime, the workshop also served as the Justice Building and the National Gallery. Near the public washrooms behind the West Block once stood a greenhouse, built in 1879.

The civil service soon outgrew its departmental buildings on the Hill proper. Extensions were made to the East and West blocks, but more office space was still needed. Thomas Fuller, architect of the Centre Block, was retained to design the Langevin Block (1883–89) on Wellington. Made of olive-green sandstone from New Brunswick, the block houses the Prime Minister's Office. It was named for Sir Hector Louis Langevin, Father of Confederation and Secretary of State between 1867 and 1869. The Confederation Building on Wellington at Bank was erected between 1927 and 1931. The sheer number of staff has not been the only reason prompting relocation from the Hill: many departments moved about five kilometres west to Tunney's Pasture because of fear of nuclear attack during the Cold War in the 1950s.

Successive governments expropriated the entire north side of Wellington Street, razing private properties to build a variety of government buildings. The promontory of cliffs overlooking the Ottawa River is currently dominated by the Supreme Court, the Justice and Confederation buildings and by the National Archives of Canada.

Because they house the federal government of Canada, the Parliament Buildings – especially the Centre Block – are used to symbolize the nation. In 1901 the Centre Block's Gothic spires were draped in black to symbolize a Dominion grieving over the death of Queen Victoria. Today the Hill is the site of public demonstrations and celebrations, and there are sound and light shows during the tourist season. The Changing of the Guard ceremony is reminiscent of the Hill's original use as a military barracks.

## Style

The Neo-Gothic spires of John A. Pearson's Centre Block, and the Gothic Revival buildings of Fuller's and Jones' original Library and Stent's and Laver's East and West blocks are stylistically sympathetic. The Gothic style, popular in its revivalist form in the mid to late 1800s, represented "the highest expression of man's aspiration" according to Canadian poet William Wilfred Campbell.

*1880s view of rear of original Parliament Buildings. The old pump house is at the base of the cliffs; on the left are the first canal locks at Entrance Bay and the stone Commissariat building. NCC, M. Newton heritage file E12-024, Box 51*

Stylistic grandeur after the fashion of a great boulevard is maintained along Wellington Street. The copper châteauesque roofs of the Confederation Building, the Justice Building and the Supreme Court integrate successfully with the deep mansard roof of the Langevin Block. But although the copper roofs provide an illusion of stylistic continuity, the buildings exhibit widely diverging styles. The Supreme Court is essentially a severe interpretation of the châteauesque style with an Art Deco interior, and the Langevin Block sports ornamental Second Empire features. And, from the promontory of the Hill, across the canal, the 1991–92 Canadian Museum of Contemporary Photography, the Chateau Laurier, the twin spires of Notre-Dame Basilica, and Safdie's National Gallery complete the image of monumental grandeur befitting a capital city.

## Walk Tips

4.5 km; 2 hours.
This walk encompasses splendid vistas of the historic Ottawa River from Parliament Hill and leads you along a pathway hugging the waterfront. The circuit route includes the Parliament Buildings, the Supreme Court of Canada and the oldest standing stone building in Ottawa, the Commissariat Building, now the Bytown Museum. Most buildings are open to the public. Tours of the Centre and East Block and Supreme Court are available year round. The Bytown Museum is open May to October.

As you walk you will "meet" prominent political leaders of our past. Statues people the Hill: most recently, in 1992, Queen Elizabeth II unveiled an unusual statue of herself astride a horse. Other statues include the likenesses of Thomas D'Arcy McGee, who was murdered on nearby Sparks Street, and prime ministers Sir John A. Macdonald and William Lyon Mackenzie King.

## The Walk

Start at the Centennial Flame in the middle of the lawn directly in front of the Centre Block. Facing you is the ninety-metre-high Peace Tower, the symbolic centre of Parliament Hill, Ottawa and the nation. On your left is the West Block, on your right the East Block. The architects of these flanking buildings, Stent and Laver, did not create identical structures, yet the two lend the Hill a symmetrical composition.

First visit the **East Block**, built 1859–66 in the highly decorated Gothic Revival style. Some original features have been altered: in 1870

*East Block; note the variegated slate roof now replaced by copper.* NCC 172

dormer windows were added to the roof, wings were added between 1910–13, copper replaced the variegated slate roofs of all three government buildings in the 1940s, and in 1976–80 the Department of Public Works renovated the interior space. We can be thankful a proposal to paint the exterior stone yellow was not adopted.

Note the delicate wrought iron cresting running on top of the roof. Although the spires appear to be composed entirely of copper, it is actually this ironwork that carries your eye up to complete the Gothic spires. The ironwork lends a picturesque airiness to the overall design.

Typical of the Gothic Revival style, the exterior of the building is extremely fanciful. There are what resemble "faces" in the East Block's southwest corner tower, both at the entrance door and the second-storey. Note the dramatic keyhole effect above this tower's doorways, accentuated by the uncoursed red and yellow sandstone – a random patterning which is echoed in the East Block's window bays. Hourly tours in the summer (on weekends in winter) allow you to explore the interior.

The Prime Minister and Privy Council offices were in the East Block until 1976, when they were moved across the street into the Langevin Block. As you turn left to pass in front of the East Block, notice the carriage-porch, called the Governor General's entrance. It once led to the vice-regal offices, but they were relocated to Rideau Hall in 1942. From the times of the first governor general, Lord Monck, capital planners have wrestled with defining a ceremonial route between this office and Rideau Hall. Part of the NCC's Confederation Boulevard represents the latest attempt to provide a picturesque approach from the Hill to Rideau Hall.

Follow the curving drive to Pearson's **Centre Block** (1916–27). Pearson's Neo-Gothic design provides fascinating contrast to Stent and Laver's East and West blocks. Pearson's rendering of the Gothic style is far more restrained, and despite exterior ornamentation in the form of gargoyles and grotesques, the Centre Block conveys a more solid, imposing presence.

Yet Pearson's **Peace Tower** entryway is inspired by Victorian Gothic fancy. It is here that Pearson allowed his design to echo the flanking blocks. Elaborate tracery surrounds the imposing front doorway which is dramatically guarded by a rampant lion and unicorn. The tower was renovated in 1981, and the once airy lookout was enclosed by curved plexiglass. It is well worth going up the tower to experience one of the most remarkable views of the city. In fact, the public tours of the Centre Block introduce you to many of its interior delights such as the Senate and Memorial Chambers. In addition, you can continue a tradition by watching Parliament in session from the public galleries. Tours are the best way of experiencing the majesty of

Parliament's interior Gothic spaces and the intricacy of the Centre Block's elaborate stone carvings.

Once inside its oak and brass doors, you enter a world of lush Gothic detailing. Ribbed vaults, compound pointed arches, elaborately carved capitals and intricate bosses lift your eye upwards. Interior Gothic detailing continues in the foyers and chambers of the Senate and Commons. The Senate, which is carpeted in crimson and panelled in dark-stained oak is especially rich looking and features massive murals depicting scenes of World War I. But the eye is allowed repose in the Memorial Chamber, where sheer cut stone gives sudden rest and inspires thoughtful reflection.

The carvings are part of an interior and exterior project commencing in 1921 and still ongoing. Chief Parliamentary Sculptor Eleanor Milne worked on the "History of Canada" relief in the Commons Foyer. This project alone took eight years and was executed at night, while Milne worked atop a metal scaffolding.

Joining a tour is the only way you can step inside the **Parliamentary Library** which is otherwise closed to the public. It is the only surviving element of Fuller's and Jones' original design. Buttresses –

*Construction of Thomas Fuller's Parliamentary Library, c1860.* PAC-C-7374

integral structural supports – divide its ornate interior into sixteen bays, each three storeys high. Originally, the arcade galleries had glass floors. These were replaced with wood after women joined the Library staff. Ornate wrought iron balustrading coloured in matte black with gold highlights contrasts effectively with the honey-coloured maple and white pine of the walls, floor and shelves. As you step out of the Library, note the steel doors painted to resemble wood. These doors saved the Library from the 1916 fire.

Return outside and turn left (east) to circle around to the back of the Centre Block. Go to the iron fence overlooking Entrance (Sleigh) Bay and the first eight locks of the Rideau Canal. Now continue walking behind the Centre Block. You pass the original bell of Thomas Fuller and Chilion Jones' first Parliament Building, now located at the rear of the Parliamentary Library. The library's iron dome, one of the first of its kind in North America, is supported by projecting flying buttresses of Gloucester limestone. The dome was custom made in England, but had to be returned by ship several times for small adjustments, so that it would fit its space. This is no doubt one of the reasons that preliminary budgets and time estimates for the Parliament Buildings were exceeded. The architects' concept for the Library incorporated the mediaeval Gothic tradition of a polygonal-shaped Chapter House attached to English cathedrals such as Salisbury and Westminster.

Continue walking around the exterior of the Library beside the railing overlooking the Ottawa River. Look for barricaded stairs leading down the cliff face, part of the **Lovers' Walk**, closed in the Depression years due to public concern about the danger of attack from "undesirables." Farther on, you'll find the carpeted, box homes of the parliamentary cats. René Chartrand is their constant, self-appointed keeper.

Next you'll see the statue of **Queen Victoria** flanked by a lion. From here there is a spectacular view along the Ottawa River. Beyond the statue, roughly where the statue of Lester B. Pearson now stands, is the site of the original military barracks hospital.

Now walk on to the **West Block**. In 1884, Ottawa's City Clerk William P. Lett described the two blocks: "The principal material used in their construction is a hard, cream-coloured sandstone, from the adjacent Township of Nepean. The dressings, stairs, gablets, pinnacles, etc. are of Ohio free-stone, whilst a pleasing variety is given to the whole by the relieving arches of red Potsdam sandstone, over the window and door openings. The roofs are of Vermont slate, of a

*Roof of West Block on fire, 1897.* NCC 172-105

dark colour, variegated by light green bands. The marble was obtained at Arnprior, and the timber used, excepting the oak, at various localities in the Ottawa valley."[2]

The West Block was the site of the first telephone conversation in Ottawa. Prime Minister Alexander Mackenzie's private secretary, William Buckingham, recited the Lord's Prayer to him by phone in September 1877. Their success prompted immediate results: Governor General Lord Dufferin and Mackenzie authorized a two-mile telephone line from Rideau Hall, the governor general's residence, to Mackenzie's office in the West Block.

Before leaving the Hill, pause to appreciate how the Gothic design emphasizes the elevation of this lofty site. John Pearson intended his Centre Block to lead observer's eyes heavenwards. He designed the windows on each storey to be smaller than those on the storey below. The layers of gabled dormer windows are similarly designed. Finally, the narrow, pointed lancet windows in the Peace Tower pull one's gaze up to the Canadian Flag flying at its crest.

At the far corner of the West Block, turn right along its southern face and continue through the stone pillars until you emerge onto Wellington Street.

Ahead is the 1927–31 **Confederation Building,** featuring a dramatically angled, massively arched main entry complete with croisette

*Confederation Building under construction, looking northwest on Wellington from the corner of Bank, May 4, 1929. NCC, M. Newton file H12-288, Box 42*

windows. It was the first government department building built to the west of the Hill. Although it shares similar construction materials (such as sandstone and copper) with the Parliament Buildings, the Confederation Building's towers, turrets, steeply pitched roof with multiple layers of dormer windows, and its vertical massing are typical châteauesque features. Note the corbelled projection just beneath the attic (top) floor windows. This decorative motif resembles a castle, a feature you will observe later this walk in the Chateau Laurier Hotel.

Turn right (north) on the extension of Bank Street and left (west) at the next corner. You now start to walk behind the Confederation Building. Observe its interesting three-wing ground plan, and note the amount of open space used for parked cars. Periodically, there are proposals for underground parking on the Hill, but none has been adopted.

Pause in the space between the Confederation and the next large building, the Justice Building. Look left (due south) to view the Neo-Classical **Bank of Canada Building** built of granite from the Eastern Townships. The original 1937 structure, designed by Marani, Lawson and Morris, is dominated by its 1975–78 addition, the silvered glass towers of Arthur Erickson and Marani, Rounthwaite & Dick which house the bank's Central Garden Court and the Currency Museum.

*Confederation Building under construction, showing the framing of dormers in its châteauesque style roof, 1929.* NCC 172

The 1937 structure features seven vertical "bands" of windows punctuated by fluted pilasters that mimic columns. Their subdued capitals are barely visible where they meet the horizontal band of the string-course. Note how the Bank's copper roof is echoed in the 1975–79 addition: the copper was chemically aged so that it would immediately integrate with its Wellington streetscape.

To the rear of the Confederation Building there is a low white clapboard **"temporary building,"** known as the **Justice Annex.** Built during World War II to provide temporary offices, this is the survivor of three structures that once sprawled between the Supreme Court and the National Archives, ahead of you. The annex has simple colonial Georgian touches: the stylized entryway, with its columns and pediment, the wooden sash windows and the ventilator cupolas on top of the roof.

The **Justice Building** (1935) is now on your left. Architects Burritt and Horwood continued the Château style for this edifice, whose exterior is decorated by Gothic-inspired stone carvings. Note the life-size Native scout, crouched over the western entryway.

Look left (due south) again to view **St. Andrew's Presbyterian Church**, designed by architect W. T. Thomas of Montreal. The original church on this site was built by Thomas MacKay's Scottish stone-masons. This 1874 replacement features a steeple offset to the left, rather than centred above, the doorway. This reflects the Victorians' love of asymmetry. The main entryway is dramatically arched. Note how the old church is encircled by the glass curtain walls of 275–283 Sparks Street. This building, owned by the Temporal Committee of St. Andrews, houses more offices of the Bank of Canada. Its clever design emphasizes the limestone heritage church by contrasting it against the stepped, non-reflective dark brown panels inset directly behind the church. The patterns created in the modern glass towers lend an attractive "modern art" texture to Wellington Street.

Now resume your walk. Ahead is the **Supreme Court of Canada** (1937), Montreal architect Ernest Cormier's only Ottawa commission. The highest court of appeal possesses an austere, distinguished presence. Cormier emphasized this in the balanced massing of the projecting east and west towers and the massive scale of the central entry with its imposing stairs. Six column-like piers support the châteauesque copper roof and its stepped dormers. The dormers interrupt the steeply pitched roof and provide light to the interior space. Note how the sheer, unadorned cut stone walls also emphasize the building's imposing nature. Cormier was forced to change his original plans to accommodate Prime Minister King's insistence upon the châteauesque roof. As you walk towards the Supreme Court, notice the bronze statues of Justice and Truth on either side of the wide stairs, added in the 1970s. Go inside to examine the interior space.

Cormier's interior is Art Deco. The central raised classical stairway with its flanking stairs provides a suitably imposing yet balanced entry to the courtrooms. The overall effect of the interior design is of hard, shiny surfaces which demand respect: this is no unassuming or welcoming space. Only the hushed tones of lawyers (in woollen wigs) and the rich scarlet robes of the judges add a human touch.

Return outdoors and walk to the rear of the building, through the parking spaces, to discover a secluded lookout over the river from where you can look back up at Parliament Hill.

Return to the front of the Supreme Court, and continue walking west. At the intersection with Lyon pause yet again to look across Wellington to see the **East and West Memorial Buildings**, built in 1949 and 1955 respectively. Architects Allward and Gouinlock created a neo-classical façade with a suggestion of châteauesque detailing through the addition of shallow copper roofs. Lyon Street is wide where it intersects with Wellington: it used to be Upper Town's West Ward Market.

Now walk through the next park to the International Style **National Archives of Canada** (1963–67), designed by Mathers and Haldenby. The building is a departure from the Château and Gothic styles, being a series of severe monolithic blocks relieved by relentlessly marching rows of tiny windows.

Go inside as the interior space reveals the structure of this building. In the foyer you can discern the layout of its steel posts and girders beneath their finish of white marble and gilt mosaic tiles. Art and artifacts add welcome interest to the archives: Inside the main door is

*National Archives of Canada. Oct. 1991.* K. Fletcher

a bronze sculpture by Henry Moore, and murals on the second-floor reading room are by Charles Fraser Comfort, friend of the Group of Seven and the only artist to be appointed director of the National Gallery of Canada.

Return outside. Walk straight ahead to Wellington Street and pause a last time to look across the street. Look above the cascading fountain in the Garden of the Provinces to observe the stone wall delineating the western end of Sparks Street and the tall spire of **Christ Church Cathedral**. As of 1993 the congregation is raising funds to replace the deteriorating roof. Landowner Nicholas Sparks donated land for this church, first built in 1833 but completely rebuilt in 1872–73 to the design of architect King Arnoldi. The rough Nepean sandstone animates its exterior, as do the stepped gables which also accentuate the verticality of its position atop the hill. Its steeple stands in counterpoise to the spires of Parliament Hill.

Now turn right on Wellington and find the path leading down to the parking lot to the west of the archives. Walk down and look for the steps leading around the "porch" of the rear wing. These will take you to the rear of the archives, where you will find a statue of Arthur G. Doughty, Dominion Archivist 1904–35. Descend the stairs to the parking lot, and join the waterfront pathway running east towards Entrance Bay and the canal locks. To your left (west) is the Portage Bridge to Hull, Quebec, and beyond it, farther west, lie the Chaudière Falls. Pause here.

Juxtaposed to the modern Portage Bridge and the four grey staggered complexes of **Place du Portage** (1969–79) in Hull is Victoria Island's four-storey Ottawa Carbide Company Mill, built in the 1890s by Canadian inventor Thomas Leopold Willson. Between the pathway and Victoria Island is a small spit of land once known as Bellow's Landing. This was the earliest settlement of Bytown, where travellers and voyageurs caught a breath of hospitality and a bite of warm food at Mother Firth's Tavern. In September 1818 this was where four hundred disbanded soldiers from the 99th and 100th Regiments alighted. They renamed it **Richmond's Landing**, after the Duke of Richmond, the popular governor general who later tragically died from the bite of a rabid fox. The men quickly built log cabins or sheltered in tents. Their goal was to build a road to the Jock River and settle there on the free land the Crown had given them as soldiers. Afraid of a repeat of the War of 1812 with the States, the British government gave grants of free land to trained army personnel and their families. The Richmond Road, as it became known, was one of the earliest roads built in Upper Canada, and the first in Carleton County.

Now walk east along the river with the cliffs of Parliament Hill on your right. Throughout the years there have been a variety of proposals for their development, including designer-built condominiums. The path meets the start of the Rideau Canal at Entrance Bay. It was first christened Sleigh Bay, by the founder of Hull, Philemon Wright in 1818. The name commemorated his son's mid-winter wedding. Being from Perth, the Justice of the Peace had no licence to wed the couple in Wrightsville (Hull), in Lower Canada. Undaunted, the wedding party bundled up in furs and dashed over the ice in their smart horse-drawn sleighs. The couple were married in the shelter of this bay – in Upper Canada.

On the near side of the locks is the **Commissariat** building built in 1827 of limestone quarried from the adjacent cliffs. Its front gable and low pitched roof are characteristic of its Scottish stonemasons. Thomas MacKay and John Redpath, contractors for the Rideau Canal, offered this construction tender to Colonel By: "Estimate of a Stone Store to be built at the Entrance of the Rideau Canal ... The length to be 74 feet in height, the foundations to be four feet deep in the ground

*1913 view of the entry locks, Alexandra Bridge, Canadian Pacific and Hull Electric Railway Entrance to Union Station. A steamer is docked at the wharf below Major's Hill Park.* NCC 172-376

and to be 3 feet thick, the first Story [sic] to be 2 feet 6 inches thick, the remainder 2 feet thick, to be done of the best Ruble [sic] Masonry with good oak frames round all openings."

The building has a rich past, being variously a military supply warehouse, military museum, and during the late 1800s, an apartment. Tenants Auclair and Seed were a nuisance; complaints were lodged about the former because he allowed his fifty free-range chickens to eat lawn seed, and against Seed because he encouraged his children to throw stones and tamper with the lock mechanisms. Since 1951 the **Bytown Museum** has operated from the Commissariat, the oldest stone building in Ottawa.

Continue up the hill, observing the operations of the eight locks. At the last lock, you pass the 1888 lockmaster's house, also built of rough-hewn limestone. The digging of the canal posed continual problems to Pennyfather, the contractor in charge of excavation, because the walls repeatedly collapsed. Two workers died during blasting, a fate all too common for the itinerant workers, many of whom had no proper instruction in the use and science of explosives. Thomas MacKay was the masonry contractor: his team of stonemasons completed the channel for the entry locks in 1832. The massive

*Mouth of the Rideau Canal, from Parliament Hill. Engraving, 1882, from* Picturesque Canada, *by Schell and Hogan.* NCC 172

limestone blocks were quarried by MacKay's labourers from the cliffs you see surrounding Entrance Bay. In 1993, the exterior limestone slabs were removed and cracks in the canal's walls cemented. The excavation was then stabilized by brick and the exterior facing of limestone replaced.

Before climbing the stairs ahead of you to rejoin Wellington Street, stop to look left. Crowning the opposite cliff is the long, tunnel-like western façade of the **Canadian Museum of Contemporary Photography**. It opened on May 6, 1992, and was designed by the architectural firm of Rysavy & Rysavy. Indiana sandstone was imported for its exterior to match the sheer cut-stone walls of the 1908–12 Chateau Laurier Hotel directly above it. Look up the façade of the hotel to note the corbelling below its attic (top) storey. This echoes the projecting corbel of the Confederation Building you viewed earlier on this tour.

Now climb the stairs to Wellington Street and look over the bridge for an aerial view of the locks. A short walk right (west) from the top of the stairs returns you to the Parliamentary precinct and the Centennial Flame, the start of this tour.

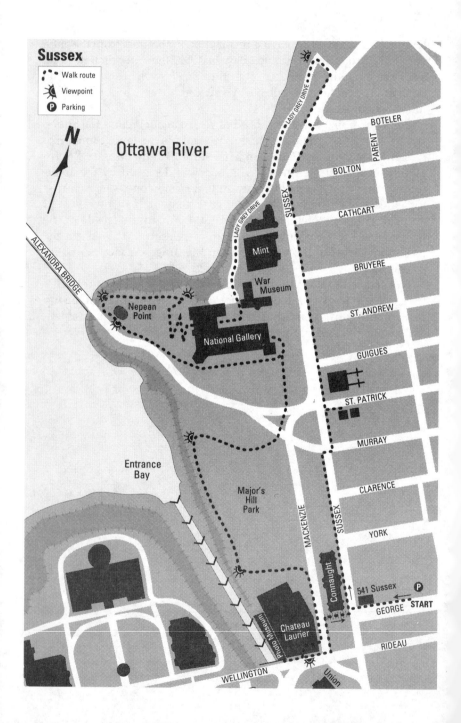

# Sussex

## History

In Ottawa's early days, Major's Hill Park and Nepean Point represented two valuable pieces of land that shared the cliff top with Barracks Hill (Parliament Hill). If military action was necessary, the canal below would serve to transport troops or goods. And so the strategic cliffs overlooking the Ottawa River were reserved for the Crown under Ordnance control.

Not coincidentally, Colonel By built his residence on Colonel's Hill (now Major's Hill), beside Entrance Bay. In June 1827, Lieutenant Pooley and Colonel By were living in homes overlooking the Commissariat. A footpath linked the Colonel's house to the Engineers' Yard at the corner of Rideau and Sussex Streets. The little path became a well-travelled lane and then Mackenzie Street, along which tradesmen in their horse-drawn wagons made pickups and deliveries at the back entries of the growing businesses along Sussex. As Sussex

*c1855 drawing of Lowertown showing McArthur's British Hotel, front centre with widow's walk on top.* NCC, M. Newton file H12-28, Box 43

*Construction of the first Canal Lock, the Steamer Wharf and the Alexandra (Interprovincial) Bridge. Harmer photograph, 1899. NCC, M. Newton file E12-003, Box 40*

Street and Lowertown grew into the commercial hub of Ottawa, the west side of Sussex was built up. Prior to 1843 most Sussex Street buildings were wooden.

Farther east on the north side of Rideau at William stood the wooden civilian barracks housing MacKay's Scottish stonemasons and their families. The barracks were luxurious in comparison to the squalid homes of the "dispensable" itinerant labourers in Lowertown, who were predominantly Irish or French Roman Catholics. The contractors had the Clerk of the Works, John MacTaggart, to speak for them: "Every care should be taken with respect to the comfort of the contractors and their people; they will have places near the works … whereon the temporary buildings may be erected … so that every person will be safely sheltered, and no time lost in coming and going to the works."[3]

Colonel By tried to assist the labourers "who had been wounded by the accidental explosion of mines, and the caving in of earth, [and who] were suffering dreadfully from being frost bitten owing to the utter impossibility of keeping them warm in the miserable log huts in which they were laying."[4] Human misery abounded in those early years. Despite Colonel By's personal intervention, the squatters and labourers did not enjoy consideration from the Ordnance Board.

Ordnance leasing of land prevented freehold ownership, and landlords who rented premises to tenants were loathe to erect permanent buildings of brick or stone lest the properties be confiscated by the government. As well, wood was readily available for the frame or log buildings, which were easily built, unlike stone or brick buildings, which required skilled tradespeople, building contractors and sometimes the design of an architect.

As Ordnance control diminished after the Vesting Act was passed in 1844, stone and brick buildings were erected on either side of the street, reflecting the confidence of freehold ownership.

The 1854 MacTaggart Street Station of the Bytown and Prescott Rail received freight just north of Cathcart Street. Later, the railway became the St. Lawrence and Ottawa prior to being absorbed by the Canadian Pacific Railway. Steamboats brought goods from Montreal to the wharves at the foot of the cliffs. By the 1850s Sussex Street was a thriving commercial centre as merchants sold the gamut of goods from local products to imported luxuries from Europe and Asia.

*Sussex at Rideau, c1865. Note horse cab stand at corner, the Chapel of Ease on west side Sussex fronting George St., the British Hotel with three-tiered verandah, and streetcar tracks.* PAC-12527

When work started on the Parliament Buildings in 1859, Ottawa's military encampment on Barracks Hill had to be moved. James Skead, owner of the British Hotel at the corner of Sussex and George offered his premises to the army. Skead and his partner had completed a major three-storey extension 132 feet along George Street to the rear of the original hotel fronting Sussex. On March 1, 1866, the British Hotel was officially accepted as the new barracks' location. It remained a barracks for four years.

In November 1866, the Champagne Hotel – later the LaSalle Academy and now Canada Mortgage and Housing Corporation offices – also became a barracks. And, on September 9, 1867, the Nun's General Hospital, at the corner of Sussex and Bruyère, became another. Until the permanent removal of Imperial troops from Ottawa in August 1870, Sussex was a military enclave. This was the period of the threatened Fenian Invasions.

In the decade between 1857 and 1867, Ottawa's population more than doubled, from 7,760 to 18,700, due to the growth of the civil service and accompanying infrastructure of business services. This influx of people started a boom of building and renovation, and

*British Hotel after 1880, showing Thomas Askwith's addition fronting Sussex and James Skead's rear extension of 1865 along George Street. NCC, NCP 9747*

affected such seemingly mundane details as the building of sewers and drains.

Poor drains and a basement full of smelly water perennially plagued the British Hotel, and the location of the latrines at the General Hospital caused considerable ill feeling between the residents of Cathcart Street, the Nuns, the City's Board of Health – and the troops. The concern was the siting of the latrines: first adjacent to the wall surrounding the Nun's enclosed gardens, and then near the residents' wells. Colonel P. J. MacDougal wrote a letter summing up his annoyance over such "details": "It is a great bore but I think it will be better to meet the feelings of the people, unreasonable though they are."

After the departure of the troops in 1870, the temporary barracks reverted to their owners. Number 541 Sussex Street, the British Hotel, continued to be the cornerstone of the street. It briefly served as the Clarendon Hotel, then in 1880 the federal government purchased it. The cover of *The Canadian Illustrated News*, March 20, 1880, depicts the Marquis of Lorne opening an art exhibition in the building – a collection that, under his patronage, became the forerunner of today's National Gallery.

In September 1880, Thomas Askwith, a local contractor, demolished the original 1838–51 section of the hotel and rebuilt it using limestone from the east side of Entrance Bay. It became the Geological Museum. The museum remained until 1912, when a succession of government departments took over. It is now maintained – as is the bulk of the Sussex façade – by the National Capital Commission.

In 1874, Major's Hill was already established as a popular public park. That year it was declared the first park in Ottawa and renamed the Dominion Park by the Ottawa's City Council. In 1875 a flurry of improvements was made, including the infill of sunken areas and the building of a stone wall to prevent strollers from falling down the cliff. A glass pavilion was built, and many fountains, ornamental pools and pathways attracted visitors. In 1885 control of the park reverted to the federal government and the old name of Major's Hill was re-adopted.

The erection of the Parliament Buildings in 1865 led many to call for a ceremonial route to link Parliament with Rideau Hall. Lord and Lady Aberdeen raised the idea. Lady Aberdeen's diary entry of November 19, 1898, reveals how the couple encouraged Prime Minister Sir Wilfrid Laurier. "Look fifty years ahead and get a plan made whereby such a scheme may ultimately be developed and which will prevent eye-sores of buildings being put up." It was in this spirit that

*View of Parliament Buildings from Major's Hill, drawn by F. B. Schell, showing noon-day gun. From* Picturesque Canada *by G. M. Grant, 1882.* NCC 172

their successors, the Mintos, encouraged the construction of the iron and steel Minto Bridges across the Rideau River, in the hope that King Edward would become a grand boulevard. But King Edward Avenue abutted Rideau Street, and even in the late 1800s, this was a congested traffic area. The proposal was turned down. However, Laurier's Liberal government established the Ottawa Improvement Commission (OIC), the first of several commissions to grapple with the planning of the capital.

Although many politicians and citizens since the Aberdeens have shared their dream of a ceremonial route to link Rideau Hall to Parliament, the road was never built. By 1867, Confederation year, the city was booming. Colonel By's grid layout of lots and his survey of arterial routes had made provision for grand boulevards, but these were out of step with the reality of the city's growth. Even then, expropriation, demolition and other costly nightmares prevented the grand scheme.

The issue continues to dog successive governments and city planners. Jacques Gréber's 1951 Master Plan recognized the need for such a route, as does the NCC of the 1990s. Today, the NCC is promoting a ceremonial route, which they call "Confederation Boulevard," marked by special street signs featuring a red maple leaf. The boulevard forms a circuit route spanning the Ottawa River, joining Ottawa to Hull. Visitors pass the Peacekeeping Monument and the National Gallery on Sussex, the Parliament Buildings on Wellington and the Canadian Museum of Civilization in Hull. An offshoot of this 1992 ceremonial route links Rideau Hall to Parliament via Sussex Street.

Since 1912 the federal government has increased its presence along Sussex Street. The lovely old stone Chapel of Ease (St. John the Evangelist Church) opposite the Geological Museum burned in 1912. The government took over the site and started expropriation of all properties on the west of Sussex. A long wooden workshop extending from the Connaught Building to St. Patrick Street was erected for stonemasons employed on the rebuilding of Parliament after the 1916 fire on the Hill. It was soon demolished and the site became a parking lot. During World War II, another series of inappropriately named "temporary buildings" were erected and remained until 1979.

Between January 1961 and March 1962 the NCC expropriated most properties on the east side of Sussex from George Street north to St. Patrick – except those owned by religious institutions. This acquisition precipitated years of restoration and preservation, which have transformed Sussex into its present grand streetscape.

## Neighbourhood Styles

The restoration of Sussex's façade resulted in its designation as a historic preservation district. High-rise development is now controlled by strict zoning to conserve the heritage quality of Sussex Drive. A striking example of these efforts in the 1960s and 1970s is the preservation of the free space surrounding the tall twin Gothic spires of Notre-Dame Basilica. Its silhouette dominates not only Sussex but all of Lowertown West, reflecting the historic importance of the Roman Catholic Church in the development of the city. (The corresponding silhouette of Christ Church Cathedral on Sparks Street is muted by the high-rise development behind it.)

The architectural styles visible on this walk vary dramatically, and many buildings along the Sussex and Mackenzie loop are noteworthy, especially Skead's British Hotel, the Gothic Revival spires of the Basilica and David Ewart's fortress-like triptych, the Connaught Building, the War Museum and the Mint. The Italianate style is shown in several shopfronts along Sussex, whose arched arcades and horizontal stringcourses enliven the streetscape. Balancing these heritage sites is the modern architectural vision of Moshe Safdie's National Gallery of Canada. Anchoring Sussex at Rideau is the châteauesque

*Sussex façade at corner of George prior to the NCC's 1960s heritage conservation and urban renewal project. (Note third storey on 541 Sussex is now gone, to restore the building to Askwith's 1880 façade.)* NCC, M. Newton file, H12-350

Chateau Laurier Hotel and the classical form of Union Station. This walk presents you with the capital's most richly varied built environment.

**Walk Tips**

4 km; 2 hours.
The Sussex–Mackenzie loop is a grand introduction to the capital, for its many lookouts reveal other neighbourhoods you can explore later on. There are many public buildings to see and some, such as the National Gallery, deserve repeated visits. The gallery is of special heritage note because it houses the carefully reconstructed interior of the Rideau Street Convent Chapel.

**The Walk**

Park in the public parking lot between York and George streets. Find George Street and walk due west to Sussex. Cross at the lights so you are on the west side of Sussex. This will allow you to look down Sussex's east façade.

*Looking north along Sussex from George. Note the horse trough donated by the Aberdeens in 1893.* NCC 172-175

Stop and turn around to face **541 Sussex**, Skead's old **British Hotel**, once the Geological Museum and today home to shops, galleries and offices. Regularly spaced windows are framed by mouldings with a prominent central keystone. The cornice is supported by sturdy wooden brackets. A prominent horizontal stringcourse separating the first and second floors provides a continuum around the entire structure. The doorway has a large overhead fanlight (transom) with sidelights on either side. Corner quoins in raised cut stone further enhance this grand old building. At the rear are courtyards where guests' horses, wagons and carriages were once stabled.

George Street is wide at its junction with Sussex. In the middle of George Street there used to be a popular public well, which was first opened in 1840; a pump and cover were installed three years later. In 1893 the Aberdeens donated a watering trough, visible in many old photographs of this corner.

Turn around on Sussex and head north, staying on the west side of the street so that you can view the restored brick and limestone buildings extending as far as the twin spires of Notre-Dame Basilica, at St. Patrick Street.

Find **489 Sussex**, the former **Institut Jeanne d'Arc**, which starts at York Street. The nuns vacated the premises in 1990 ending a century's tenure. The sisters were well known for their needlework and lace-making in addition to their good works of charity and teaching. They once owned the block between York and Clarence. The oldest building is at the northern end: Colonel Joseph Aumond built his brick Revere Hotel here in 1849. Starting in 1919, the nuns purchased over a few years all five buildings in the block for a women's residence. The three to the south are of limestone; the two to the north are yellow brick. Look for the joinery distinguished by stone quoins, projecting firewalls and changes in roof level. The future of these Institute buildings is still up in the air: a $12 million restoration plan by the NCC fell through in 1992.

Between Clarence and Murray lies **449 Sussex**, formerly the **Castor Hotel**. In days gone by, when illiteracy was far more prevalent, businesses depended upon visual aids as references. The carved wooden beaver ("castor" is French for "beaver"), is still displayed here. Originally built around 1865 for François-Xavier Lapierre, the hotel became the property of Edmond Chevrier in 1877. For years it was Monette's barber shop, sporting the gay red, white and blue striped column announcing his trade. The present brick building was rebuilt by the NCC in 1978 after the original design featuring a steeply pitched roof with dormer windows. Iron guard rails march around the edge of the roofs to thwart cascades of snow from falling on passers-by. Sometimes, in winter, you can see NCC workers dressed like mountaineers, connected by ropes to the roof whilst they free the rails from dangerous accumulations of snow and ice. They add an odd type of above-sidewalk "street theatre" to a Canadian winter's day.

*National Gallery of Canada. Oct. 1991.* K. Fletcher

As you approach the corner of Murray and Sussex, look for the Italianate form of **419 Sussex**. Pause to note its polychromatic façade. Slightly projecting verticals of yellow brick pilasters, which resemble stylized columns, contrast prettily with red brick walls. The ground floor arched arcade is echoed on the second and third floors by prominent window mouldings. The second-storey windows are framed by stone mouldings, while those on the third storey are brick. Tying the composition together are strong horizontal bands of string-courses. The result lends a playful animation to the streetscape.

Now look directly ahead to the Peacekeeping Monument. The design allows you to enter its wide V to experience this 1992 celebration of Canada's internationally renowned peacekeeping efforts.

From the corner of Murray and Sussex you can see Moshe Safdie's "crystal" and granite **National Gallery of Canada**. Its glassed halls reinterpret the Gothic lines of the Parliamentary Library. (We will visit the gallery later on in this walk.) Cross St. Patrick Street, staying on the left (west) side of Sussex so you can look at the Basilica from a distance.

The towering twin spires of **Notre-Dame Basilica** balance Safdie's modern gem. Look carefully at its spires, the narrow lancet windows below them and the tracery detail in the central pointed-arched and decorated window. Surprisingly, this French Gothic Revival style is not evident on the ground floor, which sports a solid classical round-headed central doorway flanked by two smaller ones. Its prominent entablature over the main entrance is a distinctive classical feature. The classical and Gothic styles are completely different, yet have been successfully combined such that the sturdy classical base effectively supports the Basilica's triumphant spires.

A small wooden church was built on Notre-Dame's site in 1832 to serve the Catholic community of Bytown. As the town prospered, so did the parish, and the modest structure became insufficient for its needs. In 1839, Father Cannon designed a new church in the solid classical design. Antoine Robillard, a local contractor, started building in 1841. Work proceeded slowly, and in 1844 Father Pierre-Adrien Telmon replaced Father Cannon. Notre-Dame not only received a new architect, but also a new style, as Telmon was enthusiastic about the Gothic revival style sweeping France at that time.

Cross Sussex Street at St. Patrick to see the Basilica close up. Unlike the other buildings on Sussex, Notre-Dame is well set back from the sidewalk, providing a grand recessed approach for its many cere-monial functions. Construction progressed for years: the twin spires were built in 1858; in 1862 the polygonal apse and the choir were added; in 1866 a wooden statue of the Virgin was positioned atop the central peaked gable fronting Sussex, between the spires; and the

*Notre-Dame Basilica. Oct. 1991.* K. Fletcher

highly detailed interior woodwork commenced in 1878. Enter the Basilica to find master sculptor Louis-Phillippe Hébert's thirty life-size images of the saints, including those of the Virgin and St. Joseph at the main altar. In the sanctuary are sixty mahogany stalls. Local gilder and wood-carver Flavien Rochon worked alongside Hébert and the woodworker Philippe Pariseau executing the exquisite interior. Now return outside.

It's worth the short walk down St. Patrick to look at the southern face of Notre-Dame. The first projecting extension is a side porch entryway. Its twin is on the north face of the church. Both were built in 1897.

Farther down the north side of the street is **143 St. Patrick**, the **Archbishop's Palace**, linked to the Basilica by a wall enclosing a private rear garden, a later addition. Built 1849–50 the Palace is attributed to architect Father Dandurand. It contained dormitories, church offices and reception rooms. The Palace was originally the private residence for Bishop Guigues, who had been consecrated as bishop earlier that year. He moved in in May 1850 from the Donnelly House on Sussex.

*142 St. Patrick, Valade House.* NCC 168-103

The Palace features a grand doorway embellished by finely detailed ironwork. An overhanging canopy is suspended by heavy iron chains. The mansard roof – one of the first of its kind in Canada – features evenly spaced dormers. The eye is drawn up by two "falsefront" parapet gables projecting from the roofline. These are balanced by oriel windows on either side of the doorway. The NCC purchased and restored the Palace in the early 1970s, after it had fallen into disrepair.

Before returning to Sussex, view the two lovingly restored Lowertown houses directly opposite the Palace.

Number **142 St. Patrick, Valade House**, sports an outstanding example of Lowertown's "cliffhanger" second-storey porches, supported by sturdy wooden brackets. It replaces the original balcony which featured the initials of its owner, Dr. François-Xavier Valade, over its central peak. The fine stone house with its offset front door was built around 1865, and the doctor used it as both home and office until his death in 1916. The home is connected to its eastern neighbour by a carriageway that once led to a rear stable.

Number **138 St. Patrick, Rochon House**, built in 1832, is the former home of Flavien Rochon, master carver of the interior sanctuary stalls of Notre-Dame. He lived here 1853–97. The house is typical of 1840s' workers' houses once common in Lowertown. Although many have suffered the horrors of modern "improvements" such as angelstone cladding and aluminum siding, you can still find examples of well restored wooden homes if you explore Lowertown proper.

Rochon House was originally a simple rectilinear design with a central living room and kitchen and sleeping quarters upstairs. The back addition was put on between 1851 and 1878 causing the removal of rear dormers. The addition contained a new kitchen, giving extra living space at the front.

Leave St. Patrick's Street for later exploration (*see* Lowertown walk) and rejoin Sussex. Turn right (north) and proceed past the Basilica to **373 Sussex** on the corner of Guigues. Once the **Champagne Hotel**, then the **LaSalle Academy**, the building now houses the offices of Canada Mortgage and Housing Corporation. Built in 1852 as the Collège de Bytown founded by the Oblate Fathers, this is the cradle of today's University of Ottawa. By 1856 these premises were bursting at the seams, and the school moved to land donated by Sandy Hill's landowner, Louis Théodore Besserer, at the corner of Wilbrod and Cumberland. The building here on Sussex became the Champagne Hotel, later used as military barracks for the 100th Regiment at

*365 Sussex, Donnelly House.* NCC 361

the time of the Fenian threats in the mid-1860s. The hotel was well situated, being the closest to the MacTaggart Street Railway station.

Originally the building had a deeply recessed central doorway with two balconies. This feature was filled in by the Christian Brothers, who purchased the hotel in the 1870s for a parish school, which they named the LaSalle Academy in 1888. Today's prominent cupola perched upon the mansard roof was erected in 1974, replacing a series of such adornments whose last version had been removed in 1913.

Next door is **365 Sussex**, the **Donnelly House**. Built in 1844 by Irishman Thomas Donnelly as his private residence, it is a classically inspired limestone townhouse. Notice the raised end gables, a feature intended to retard the spread of fire from one wood frame roofline to another. Bishop Guigues rented the home from Donnelly while his palace at Notre-Dame was being built.

Over the years the house suffered many alterations which ended up nearly destroying the old home. In 1974 architect John Leaning was hired to restore this picturesque residence. Note the pretty transom window above the door, an elliptical Adamesque fanlight that allows light into the interior hall.

On the opposite side of Sussex find **300–350 Sussex**, the **Canadian War Museum**, designed by David Ewart. Built 1904–07 to house the Dominion Archives of Canada, the function of the building possibly dictated Ewart's choice of the sturdy Elizabethan style. Here the style is characterized by a horizontal massing, accentuated by dominant stringcourses (longitudinal bands) between storeys, projecting symmetrical bays and evenly spaced windows. These croisette windows have stone mullions (vertical) and transoms (horizontal) – both typical Elizabethan features. The main entry is set in a projecting bay tower. The building's design speaks of solid grandeur, befitting its lives as national archives and war museum. The wing on the left by Band, Burritt, Meredith and Ewart was added in 1924. It integrates fairly well, but lacks the detail of Ewart's original design.

Continue north on Sussex. Between St. Andrew and Bruyère the streetscape is relieved by a small green park which hides a parking lot behind. At the corner of Sussex and Bruyère is the **Mother House of the Grey Nuns (the Sisters of Charity),** founded in 1845 by Mère Elisabeth Bruyère. The south wing of the convent was built in 1849 by the same Antoine Robillard who built the classical base of Notre-Dame. The northern wing, on the corner of Sussex and Cathcart, came later, built as St. Joseph's orphanage in 1866. A recessed addition, built in 1885, connects the first two buildings. The 1930s witnessed the unfortunate removal of the original hipped, tin-plate roof. A fourth storey was added at this time. A low wall fronts the convent on Bruyère and is continued north along Sussex to screen the gardens from public view. This section of the wall was repointed and stabilized in 1992.

*David Ewart's Royal Canadian Mint, 1905.* NCC, M. Newton file, H12-138

Across the street is **320 Sussex**, the **Royal Canadian Mint**, architect David Ewart's 1905–08 castellated masterpiece. Resembling a fortress, it assures onlookers that the nation's currency is well protected. In the 1980s it was dismantled, its stones numbered, and carefully rebuilt to accommodate a major interior refurbishing. The Mint's buttressed walls look like battlements and sport turrets complete with slits for imaginary archers. Its Elizabethan styling includes box-shaped label mouldings surrounding the windows in a completely different fashion than the curved Italianate mouldings that framed the windows of 419 Sussex.

Continue along Sussex as it curves to the east, passing Cathcart Street. At the corner is a large brick residence, followed by a small apartment building and single house. They are of note as the only remaining residences along this entire stretch of Sussex Drive. Proceed to Boteler Street, following the curve of Sussex, and cross over to what is now the north, or Ottawa River side, of the street. Turn left (west) to follow the curve back to **Lady Grey Drive**.

This drive descends to the river. An early Bytown road, it was extended by the OIC as a possible link between Parliament and Rideau Hall – the extension was an unpopular failure. Steamship wharves once lined this stretch of the waterfront. First built by Colonel By in 1827 to receive supplies needed by his Royal Engineers to build the Rideau Canal, the docks were closed in 1901 when the Alexandra Bridge (also known as the Interprovincial Bridge) was built. At the end of Lady Grey Drive, climb the staircase on your left, which leads to the Curatorial Wing of the National Gallery. At the top you can see the rear of Ewart's Canadian War Museum with its English Tudor Rose and French fleur de lis motifs carved in the stone.

Turn to your right and follow the passageway between the wings of the National Gallery to **Nepean Point**. Up the grassy slope find the rather obscure lookout point directly to your right, at the end of the gallery, which overlooks Lady Grey Drive and the Ottawa River. From here there is a superb eastern view of the large span of the **Macdonald-Cartier Bridge**, named after the two politicians most dedicated to Confederation. It is the largest box girder bridge in Canada, built 1963–65.

Just beyond it lies **Earnscliffe**, which you can identify by its white bargeboard (gingerbread) trim beneath a steeply pitched, gabled roof. Today its Union Jack flag claims it as the residence of the United Kingdom's High Commissioner. The 1857 English Gothic cottage, built for canal contractor Thomas MacKay's daughter Annie and his son-in-law, John MacKinnon, was Sir John A. Macdonald's last home. He died here in 1891. Sarah Grimason, one of the prime minister's Kingston constituents, was a visitor to Earnscliffe in 1889. Her letter describes the Macdonald residence: "They do have a lovely place all their own, down by the Rye-do. The house has a lovely slate roof like they have in England, and beautiful grounds and a man to wait on the dure [sic: door]. Lady Macdonald keeps her own cow and hins [sic: hens] and they make their own butter. ... They have two fine cows and six servants."[5]

Beyond Earnscliffe lie the National Research Council and the French Embassy, bordering Rideau Falls. You can also see the horizontal layers of red precast concrete and smoked glass of the **Lester B. Pearson building (External Affairs)** on the south side of Sussex.

Now turn left and, keeping the cliff edge with its iron fence on your right, climb the hill to the promontory overlooking the western section of the Ottawa River. From here you can see the **Portage Bridge** in the distance, linking Ottawa to the **Place du Portage** complex in Hull, named for the old portage around the Chaudière Falls used by the Algonquin, Huron and Iroquois peoples. Beyond it are the falls, bridge and mills of the Chaudière. Once the falls were harnessed for their generating power, Lowertown's markets and the New Edinburgh mills gave way to an emerging, increasingly prominent Centre-

*View of Nepean Point from Peace Tower, 1948.* NCC, M. Newton file L-12-001, Box 54

town development. By the 1880s and into the early 1900s, the Chaudière was producing millions of board feet of sawn lumber and employing about 300 men. Lumber was stacked in huge piles: they became the tinder for the fire of 1900.

On the Hull side of the river are the dramatically sinuous curves of the **Canadian Museum of Civilization** (1989). Douglas Cardinal's building is, as he has said, "of nature." Its flowing lines not only echo the rolling Gatineau Hills in the background, but also the swirling eddies and currents of the Ottawa River. Similarly, its multi-layered storeys effectively mimic the cliffs of the Hill and Nepean Point on the Ontario side. Its design is reminiscent of Frank Lloyd Wright's organic style of architecture. However, Cardinal's aboriginal heritage is also at work here. Despite its striking contrast in style, Cardinal's museum is a fitting companion to its architectural mates: the National Gallery and the Parliament Buildings. It is the crowning jewel of the Hull side of the NCC's Confederation Boulevard.

Below you are the cantilevered spans of the **Alexandra Bridge** built in 1900 by the Dominion Bridge Company of Montreal, which also built the Chaudière Bridge in 1914. The Alexandra was built for two railways: the Pontiac and Pacific Junction (known as the "Push, Pull and Jerk") and the Gatineau Railway: the first linked the capital with Pontiac County, west of Hull, the latter ran from Ottawa to Wakefield. The left side of the bridge is a boardwalk of wooden planks, the central lane is the original rail track, and its easternmost lane is the route north to Hull. The railway tracks were removed in 1967.

Now head down the hill towards the National Gallery. You pass by a statue of Champlain by Canadian sculptor Hamilton MacCarthy with his crouching Huron guide. Champlain is holding (upside down!) an astrolabe, which he later lost about sixty kilometres west of here during his 1613 expedition. The original astrolabe is now located in the Canadian Museum of Civilization, which you just spied, in Hull.

You now walk past architect John Leaning's **Astrolabe Theatre** built in Canada's Centennial year, 1967. Popular open air concerts still entertain visitors. On your right is one of the most beautiful panorama vistas the city has to offer of the Parliament Buildings. Continue walking east towards the National Gallery, keeping to the immediate right of its main building.

*Rideau Street Convent about 1888, now rebuilt inside Moshe Safdie's National Gallery.* NCC 172

The **National Gallery**, which opened in 1988, is well worth a visit. Its foyer is a glass-topped tower, featuring triangular "sails" of cloth which assist in temperature control of the building and reflect natural light. The foyer leads to the ramped colonnade, whose magnificent glass windows overlook Parliament Hill. Architect Moshe Safdie has designed the building so that the public spaces wrap around the galleries.

In true post-modernist style, Safdie reinterprets traditional design elements to create a structure that attempts to integrate into the historical streetscape of Sussex Drive. The polygonal "crystal" tower, for example, over the main foyer is a modern rendering of the Gothic Chapter House of Thomas Fuller and Chilion Jones' Parliamentary Library. Stylized flying buttresses along the Gallery's southern façade continue this stylistic motif.

The Gallery is of special heritage interest because it is home to the interior of the **Chapel** of the **Rideau Street Convent of Our Lady of the Sacred Heart** built 1887–88. Public opposition to its demolition was among the most heated ever in Ottawa. The defenders lost their battle – but compromise was partially gained by the chapel's careful reassembly in the gallery. Its incorporation into the gallery is appropriate, for originally it was built inside a popular pre-confederation hotel on the corner of Waller and Rideau. The Sisters of Charity commissioned this exquisite chapel. Of particular importance are its cast iron pillars which support the painted wood fan-vaulted ceiling. The pillars represent state-of-the-art European technology of the day. The delicate surface paint work on these pillars are a wonderful *trompe-l'oeil* for they integrate perfectly with the painted wood.

Outside the gallery, turn right (south) on Sussex, as it curves right onto Mackenzie and enter the shaded, grassy pathways of **Major's Hill Park**. Continue right until you arrive at the cliffs overlooking Entrance Bay, the locks, the Commissariat, the Canadian Museum of Contemporary Photography and the Parliament Buildings.

There are several historic features in Major's Hill Park, among them the noon-day gun, fired at midday from April 26, 1869 on, to advise residents of the accurate time. A little farther south lie the ruins of a house foundation. First Colonel By and then Major Bolton – after whom the park is named – lived here. The home, described as a rubble stone dwelling, had a wrap-around verandah and a spectacular view. Farther on is a statue of Lieutenant-Colonel By himself, surveying his Entrance Bay locks.

You are now approaching the rear of the **Chateau Laurier Hotel** which is best viewed from its front elevation at Rideau Street. The original section was built 1908–12 by architects Ross and MacFarlane, in the châteauesque (Château) style which had become extremely popular specifically for railway hotels across Canada.

*Chateau Laurier Hotel from Commissariat Building at full moon.* NCC 172-598

Enter this charming old hotel to view its ornately carved wooden panelling in the front foyer. Ask directions to the basement swimming pool – an Art Deco delight. A 1911 tourist guide proclaimed the hotel's advantages: "The corridors are divided into sections by means of fire doors to separate them in an emergency, although the hotel is absolutely fireproof, no wood, except frames for doors and baseboards, being used in its construction. The main corridors lead directly to fire escapes, iron balconies and stairways inside the building. All the windows and service floors will be screened with the best Canadian-made fly screens, and a special refrigerating room will be provided to freeze the garbage until it is removed from the building."[6]

*Union Station, the present Government Conference Centre, under construction, 1912.* NCC 172-149

Emerge onto the carriageway entrance on Rideau through the revolving front doors. Walk to the street level and turn around to take a close look up at the hotel which towers above you like a castle.

The strong vertical massing, typical of châteauesque buildings, is accentuated here by its sheer sandstone walls which are relatively unadorned until the top (attic) floors. The steeply-pitched copper roofline lends the hotel its most dramatic châteauesque feature. But two other motifs emphasize the castle imagery. Note the projecting corbel beneath the attic (top) storey which suddenly breaks the otherwise sheer walls of the hotel. Let your eye rise up the walls to note the crenellation atop the southwest tower. On a real castle, it is this battlement feature that allowed archers to aim their bows and shoot arrows at their foes.

Look for the projecting wall dormers that rise above the top floor and which punctuate the copper roofline. These projections are decorated by crockets that march down either side of their steep sides, and their peaks are topped with finials that carry your eye "into the sky." The castle-like atmosphere is enhanced by the corner tourelles, small towers that sport narrow slit windows as if for medieval archers.

The selection of an architect for the Chateau Laurier is shrouded in intrigue. The competition was won by Boston-born Bradford Lee Gilbert. However, he was dismissed in 1908 despite cabinet approval of his design a year earlier. It is not known why Gilbert was fired, but he was replaced by the Montreal firm of Ross and MacFarlane, who adapted his plan to the châteauesque design before you.

Included in the design was an underground tunnel linking the railway hotel to its *raison d'être*, Union Station, now the Government Conference Centre, built in 1912 by the Grand Trunk Railway. Despite a storm of controversy, created by those who thought a tunnel would attract "not only pickpockets but gentlemen whose misdemeanors were of a far more serious nature," the underground link was built – a tremendous convenience for disembarking passengers and, today, for beleaguered politicians. Interestingly, a network of underground tunnels reportedly link the hotel with Parliament Hill.

Now turn right and walk just a few paces over the bridge to look back at the **Canadian Museum of Contemporary Photography**, which opened in 1992. The limestone used in its sheer walls, was especially ordered from Indiana to match the Chateau Laurier. The design integrates with the sidewalk level of the street and closely resembles an underground subway, providing a historical link to the old railway hotel and Union Station. From the bridge, note the rhythmic pattern of arches on the museum's western face above the canal entry locks. These successfully echo the hotel's parking lot entryways. The balustraded railing along the top of the museum and the globe-lights further lighten the façade.

Now face southeast, to look at **Union Station**, today's **Government Conference Centre**. Bradford Lee Gilbert was also the original architect of Union Station, and, again, Ross and MacFarlane took over when Gilbert was dismissed, making many changes to his original design. The classical proportions and stately columns of the former station are an inspiring finalé to the foot of Sussex Drive – yet it barely survived demolition in 1965. In 1966 the tracks were torn up, the terminus and rails removed to their Alta Vista location, and in 1967 the once-proud station started a new life as the Centennial Centre and subsequently the Government Conference Centre.

Monumental Doric columns and a prominent triangular pediment are characteristic of the classical style. Look up to the top attic windows above the heavy cornice: their understated placement successfully lightens the massive presence of Union Station. The incongruous canopy suspended by huge chains over the main doorway on Rideau Street compromises the classical strength of the building.

Now turn back. Pass by the Canadian Museum of Contemporary Photography to the west of the Chateau Laurier. Walk north on Mackenzie towards the **Department of Revenue**, the **Connaught Building**, David Ewart's third proud, fortress-like government edifice on Sussex. Built 1913–14 while Ewart was chief architect of the Department of Public Works, it is a successful complement to his Mint and War Museum. (*See* Sandy Hill walk to view Ewart's completely different design for his own home.) Of all his Ottawa designs, Ewart thought this to be the best.

The massing of the Connaught Building is in the fortress style of a Scottish baronial castle. Ewart softens the overall effect by such touches as Tudor arched windows with Gothic tracery over the entrances. These, in combination with other features such as multi-storey bay windows with balconies and narrow, pointed lancet windows in the turrets of the centre tower, lighten the façade.

Just south of the Connaught Building is a staircase leading down to Sussex at George. Descend these steps to the start of the tour. Or you could walk beside the building to a second staircase on its north side. It leads down to a parking lot just north of George.

*Connaught Building, named after the Duke of Connaught, governor general from 1911–16.* PAC-PA-43766

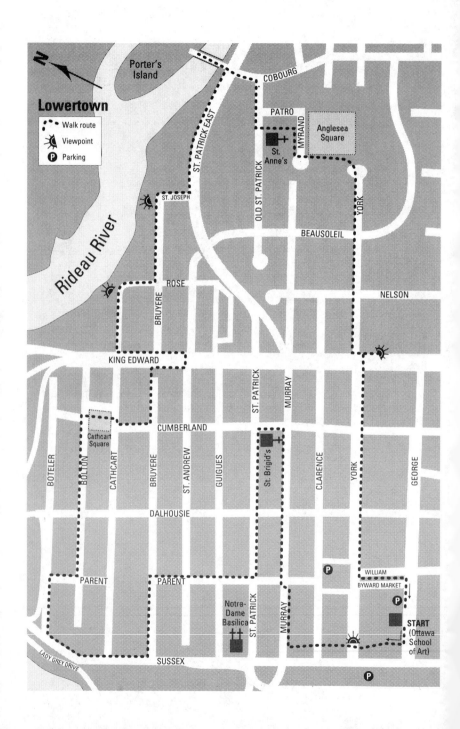

N

Porter's
Island

**Lowertown**

- ●●● Walk route
- ☀ Viewpoint
- **P** Parking

COBOURG

PATRO

Anglesea
Square

St.
Anne's

MYRAND

ST. PATRICK EAST

OLD ST. PATRICK

Rideau River

ST. JOSEPH

☀

BEAUSOLEIL

YORK

ROSE

☀

BRUYERE

NELSON

KING EDWARD

☀

Cathcart
Square

CUMBERLAND

ST. PATRICK

MURRAY

BOTELER

BOLTON

CATHCART

BRUYERE

ST. ANDREW

GUIGUES

St. Brigid's

CLARENCE

YORK

GEORGE

DALHOUSIE

P

WILLIAM

PARENT

PARENT

BYWARD MARKET

P

Notre-
Dame
Basilica

ST. PATRICK

MURRAY

☀

**START**
(Ottawa
School
of Art)

LADY GREY DRIVE

SUSSEX

P

# Lowertown

## History

Lowertown was originally an almost impenetrable cedar swamp. By 1827 Colonel By had had the area surveyed and had handed out the first lots to civil servants. At the same time he reserved land for a wide street (George Street) under which the Bywash – an outflow of the Rideau Canal – would pass. Once drained, these lands were quickly settled and log cabins and other wooden buildings were erected. Until the Vesting Act of 1844 was passed, land speculation was rife in Lowertown, rents to the Crown varied unfairly, and there

*The bustle of York Street, c1902. On the left side is the Grant Building, 1901, with "Joseph Grant, Grocer" sign painted on its brick wall. Also, with its dormers piercing the third storey is 41 York, the St. Louis Hotel. First building on the right is 18 York, then the Institut canadien-français and farther along, the Lafayette House built 1849–50. NCC, M. Newton file H12-716, Box 43*

was little incentive to build more permanent dwellings. Its earliest inhabitants were labourers on the Rideau Canal, shantymen and rivermen – and their families.

A look at the reality of life for these workers perhaps explains Lowertown's rowdy reputation. Canal workers were unemployed during the winter months, and shantymen were idle in summer. Without welfare or other means of support they eked out a living in Lowertown. The fate of a widowed woman with children was appalling: if her husband died – or was maimed on the job – she had little choice but to turn to prostitution as the means of support. And so the rhythm of Lowertown established itself in its formative years.

In its earliest years, Lowertown was a boisterous, unlawful part of Bytown, bounded by Besserer's Sandy Hill estate to the south; the Ordnance Lands (reserve "O") extending to Rideau Falls to the northeast; Major's Hill, Barracks Hill and the Canal Reserve to the west, and Nicholas Sparks' land (Upper Town) south of Wellington. Unease in the settlement festered in 1832, 1834 and again in 1847 with the influx of desperately ill Irish immigrants. These were the years of typhus and cholera, sicknesses that ravaged Bytown's populations.

*Workers at 13–15 Clarence St., A. Thibert, Carriage Builder, 1914.* NCC, M. Newton file, H12–184

The Grey Nuns came to Lowertown from Montreal in 1845 to minister to its poor and sick residents. The pitiful state of the Irish immigrants, who arrived early in 1847 famine-weary and full of typhus, generated an outpouring of concern and care. The nuns organized doctors and ministers of all denominations and arranged for the building of shelters for the sick and dying. The Immigrant Hospital was located near the Grey Nuns' residence on Bruyère at Sussex. After the epidemic, no one wanted to buy or to reside in it, so great was the fear of contagion.

Just as the Irish vied with the French-Canadians for employment, so did educated and moneyed residents of Upper Town vie with the rapidly expanding population of Lowertown. Arguments raged over the location of the city hall, post office – and market. The 1836 brawls between Irish Shiners and their French counterparts, such as legendary hero Joseph Montferrand, were echoed by the struggles for power of the upper and middle classes' politicians and businessmen.

For economic reasons, the siting of the market between George and York streets was critical. First water transportation routes, then rail, in the location of the Bytown and Prescott Railway Station on McTaggart Street (1854), gave Lowertown the edge.

Upper Town residents looked askance at booming Lowertown and fretted that this upstart group would dominate their traditional power base. Politically the two groups were adversaries: Upper Town was a Tory Protestant stronghold, Lowertown the dominion of the Reformers. In September 1849, Bytown was rocked by civil insurgence pitting Tory against Reformer in the September 1849 insurrection called Stoney Monday. A stone-throwing mêlée, complete with gunshots, in Market Square left twenty-nine men injured and one man dead. The next Wednesday saw further insurrection. A thousand Reformers armed with canon and firearms from Philemon Wright's Hull armoury faced 1,700 Tories similarly fortified. Between them, on the Sappers Bridge, stood a military attachment from Barracks Hill. Reason prevailed, no battle ensued, and the day ended peacefully.

After the incorporation of Bytown in 1850, Lowertown was dealt several blows which shifted most of the activity and commerce of its bustling market and attractive Sussex promenade of shops to Upper Town. The harnessing of the Chaudière Falls was one factor. The second was Queen Victoria's choice of Ottawa as capital – and the subsequent siting of the Parliament Buildings on Barracks Hill. Upper

Town gained prominence as businesses vied for addresses adjacent to the seat of power.

But Lowertown did continue to grow and prosper. Today its colourful farmer's market, and its varied streetscape of shops, public buildings and residences give Lowertown a vibrant life all its own.

## Neighbourhood Styles

"Sir, – If we want to have a nice town we must pass a by law to prevent people building those one and two storey shanties as on Rideau Street, near Dalhousie. I think it a disgrace to have such buildings in our town. In future let them do better and go out to the bush and build their shanties for the owls to see."[7]

So wrote "lover of architecture" John Pink in 1888. He would be surprised to learn his concerns are echoed in the Lowertown of the 1990s. Ottawa's oldest section of town still arouses hearty debate as property owners, developers and politicians struggle with issues such as density, height restrictions and heritage conservation.

Until the Vesting Act of 1844, which released Ordnance land to private ownership, buildings of any permanence were rare. Stone represented wealth and permanence – both features being stranger to many Lowertown residents. Only on Sussex Drive, Lowertown's

*York St. looking east from Sussex, Oct. 1991. Compare with the c1902 photo of York St.: all buildings remain.* K. Fletcher

western boundary, were the buildings quite grand from an early date: the Basilica was started in 1841, the Bruyère Hospital in 1849. (*See* Sussex walk)

Then, on May 10, 1860, a new city by-law prohibited the building of wooden structures in designated parts of Ottawa, notably opposite the Parliament Buildings and also in Lowertown, along Sussex, York and George Streets. The old log and frame homes were eventually replaced or were clad with brick, pressed tin, angel stone and, more recently, aluminum siding as technology and residents' means improved.

## Walk Tips

6 km; 3 hours.
This is a long walk introducing you to both Lowertown East and West. Many public buildings can be explored both inside and out – a great benefit on cold or wet days. The market is fun to explore: there's lots to see and do and many a street corner offers much for the eyes, ears – and stomach – to feast upon. (Detailed descriptions of the Sussex façade, Notre-Dame Basilica, the Donnelly House and LaSalle Academy are given in the Sussex Walk. However, because their influence dominates Lowertown, they are briefly mentioned here.)

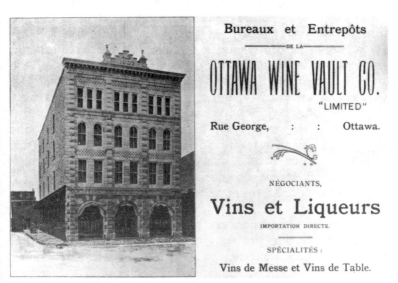

*Advertisement with date 1907 visible on the parapet front gable. Note wooden wine casks on the left. NCC 172-375*

## The Walk

Start your walk in the Byward Market area. If you are driving, park in the public lots accessed either one block south (from York), or on George Street itself.

Number **35 George Street**, the **Ottawa School of Art**, directly across from The Bay, is the first building of note. Built in 1907, this roughcut limestone Romanesque Revival building originally housed the Ottawa Wine Vault Company. Its rounded arched windows set between pilasters form a sturdy ground floor arcade. Beneath its adjacent parking lot lay its underground vaults. Stand back to appreciate how its façade is lightened at each storey. This is achieved by a vertical progression from three large, arched storefront windows to paired windows on the second floor, to groups of three on the third. The building's verticality is emphasized even more by the column-like pilasters, while stone horizontal stringcourses bind the composition together. In 1983 it became the Ottawa School of Art's new home. The school is often open, so you may be able to view its much-altered interior and its original stone walls, still exposed in the stairwell.

Outside, turn right (west) on George Street, and once past the two stone arches, cut through a walkway just after the Café Marie Antoinette. Turn right and descend the few steps into a cobblestone courtyard, built around 1865. This is the **Clarendon Court**, which takes its name from the early hotel (whose precursor was the British Hotel, *see* Sussex walk). The courtyards are an important heritage feature of Lowertown, relics of the day when horse and wagon needed stabling and rear access to the businesses fronting the street. Today the tidy courtyard is peppered with art, benches and cafés, a reprieve from the hustle-bustle and dust of the street.

Pass through the archway on your right, stepping into the parking lot. (The photograph on the front cover of this book is taken from this spot.) Keep to your left for several paces (in the parking lot). Another courtyard entry appears on your immediate left. Enter and zig-zag through, to your right, emerging on York Street. On your immediate right is **12 York**. Its red brick façade forms an arcade sheltering a glass-enclosed office with rounded corners on the ground floor.

Next door, to your right (east), is **18 York** (1876), once the **Institut canadien-français**, then the **Château Cheese Factory**. It suffered devastating fires in 1880, 1887 and most recently in 1970, when only the exterior limestone façade was saved. Today the property is owned by the National Capital Commission. *The Ottawa Citizen* of October 6,

*George Matthew's Pork Packing Establishment at 18 York in 1892; next door is a blacksmith, J. Mahoney, and to the right is the Central Fire Station (demolished).*
PAC-PA-27270

1876, reported that it had six lofty meeting rooms in its basement, one of which held 400 people. Above it was a hall which had seating for 1,000. The Institute leased rooms to theatre companies, and even circuses performed inside its walls. In 1889, after the second fire, George Matthews bought the building for $2,850 and rebuilt the interior to accommodate a pork packing plant.

Directly across the road, on the north side of the street, is **17A York**, once "Grant's Grocery," built in 1901. Cross to the centre "island" of the road and look up the building's western façade. You can see the remnants of a painted sign, a reminder of how merchants advertised their wares in years predating neon signs, television and radio ads. Notice the alleyway entrance to the left of 17A.

Before walking through the alley beside 17A, pause to glance right (east) on York Street. It was here that Reformers ran from pursuing Tories in the Stoney Monday riot of September 1849. Some dashed into **42 York**, the **Château Lafayette**, a four-storey stone and brick hotel and watering hole operated by Francis Grant in the early 1840s. Others ran across the street to **41 York**, then the **St. Louis Hotel**, and now the Ottawa Valley Goods Store, built 1874–75. Shots rang out and a grand mêlée ensued. This is the heart of the Stoney Monday riot.

*41 York St., Oct. 1991. Its heritage restoration won an architectural merit award for owner Eric Cohen. It was a combined restoration project of architect Julian Smith, Cimmeron Development and Uniat Design Management.* K. Fletcher

Turn around and look due west and up towards Parliament. Compare modern-day York Street with this old photograph.

Now cross the road and slip into the alleyway beside 17A York Street. As you pass through this courtyard, note the five-sided bay extension. The entire block on Sussex from York to Clarence was part of the Institute Jeanne d'Arc (*see* Sussex walk). The corner building on Clarence was Colonel Joseph Aumond's 1849 brick Revere Hotel – the oldest building on the block.

You now emerge onto Clarence Street. Pause to view **13–15 Clarence**, built in 1892, and compare it to its old photograph shown here. Today the apartment entry is graced by a highly detailed wooden balcony.

Cross Clarence and enter the beautifully restored **Tin House Court**. You are walking amid the original tradesman's entrances and stables of such mid to late nineteenth century Sussex businesses as the Castor Hotel (*see* Sussex walk). Take special note of the preserved façade of roofer, contractor and tinsmith Honoré Foisy's 1905 home, now mounted on a limestone wall. It has all the appearance of a fantastical metal sculpture, but it is the actual façade of Foisy's house, which once stood at 136 Guigues Street. Tin was once a commonly used construction material as it was inexpensive and shielded the

*View of the Parliamentary Library from a congested York St.* NCC 172-213

*Inside 13–15 Clarence; A. Thibert, Carriage Builder, 1914.* NCC, M. Newton file, H12–184

building from rain, sleet and snow. As with many artisans, Foisy used his own home to advertise his considerable talents.

Continue through this enchanting courtyard. A cascading fountain enlivens the quiet mood, and park benches are conveniently placed, inviting you to stop awhile, to imagine the days of horse-drawn wagons and bustling activity that once was the life of Lowertown.

You emerge onto Murray Street. Turn right (east) and find **55 Murray**, once the **Martineau Hotel**. Named after its first owner, Eugene Martineau, the original hotel was built in 1872. The building was purchased in 1977 by the Heritage Canada Foundation. The Martineau possesses a simple Georgian classical design, with regular windows accentuating a horizontal composition. Slightly raised end gables were built to retard fire. Built of limestone, it is a good example of the handiwork of the Rideau Canal masons who passed their knowledge to their sons. Kitchens were located in four stone wings at the back. In its heyday, the Martineau, which boasted seventy rooms, was one of the most popular taverns for Ottawa River raftsmen. Inside its arched doorways, which have replaced the old carriageway entries to the rear yard, you can see how the hotel has been adapted to shops and offices. The window sills reveal the depth of the walls.

Now walk right (east) on Murray Street. Cross Dalhousie and continue until you reach **159 Murray**, the **École Guigues School**. In 1915 the Province of Ontario forbade the instruction of students in French. Rule 17 provoked a public outcry, and this school was the site of a large demonstration against the ruling. The historical plaque outside the school explains the struggle of French Canadians to ensure the survival of their language and culture. Rights were reinstated. The school continued to teach in French and reconfirmed the Franco-Ontarien reality of Lowertown.

Today, this school's fate is undetermined and demolition is a real threat. It is of symmetrical classical style, featuring regularly spaced rectangular windows with stone lintels and sills, a raised portico with flanking stairs and, surprisingly, wooden columns. The cornice unfortunately has been removed.

A few steps along is **179 Murray**, **St. Brigid's Presbytery**. Its wishbone central gable and mansard roof lends drama to the streetscape. The pillared verandah is set wide upon the front of the brick home. The 1892 home is one of Ottawa's best examples of residential Second Empire style so popular in Victorian times. The Goad insurance map of Ottawa dated 1878 shows several small wooden frame buildings on this site predating this brick home.

Continue along Murray and turn left (north) onto Cumberland, walking beside **St. Brigid's Church**, built 1889–90 as the first Roman Catholic Church in Lowertown to serve the English-speaking members of the parish. St. Anne's (in Lowertown East) and the Basilica served French Catholics. The best view of the church is from St. Patrick at the intersection ahead. Turn left (west) on St. Patrick.

Look up to examine the two spires of St. Brigid's: they are of unequal height and completely different shape. Such disparity appealed to the Victorians' delight in asymmetrical composition, which represented an exciting departure from the regular features of classicism. Together with the Basilica, these two spires are signature landmarks of Lowertown.

Although it has a Gothic interior, St. Brigid's exterior exhibits Romanesque Revival detailing, notably in its three heavy, rounded arched portals fronting onto St. Patrick Street, and its paired, round-headed windows. The colonnettes – narrow non-supporting columns on the front façade – are adorned with foliated capitals, a typical Romanesque detail.

Continue up St. Patrick, walking on the south side of the street to **288–290 St. Patrick**, **Brulé House**, built around 1842. It is a well preserved French Canadian style wooden clapboard double with steeply pitched, gable roof with dormers. It is one of the few remaining workman's doubles once common in Lowertown.

Cross Dalhousie, continuing along St. Patrick. On the south side, note **230 St. Patrick**, Johnson's, with its large tempered glass front. Its showcase window provides effective advertising to passers-by.

*The Notre-Dame Basilica and the Archbishop's Palace. Nov. 1991. K. Fletcher*

Number **224–226 St. Patrick** is a four-storey flat-top apartment block featuring an overhanging porch of finely detailed wood. Note the cornice with its wooden bracket supports. Farther along, **215 St. Patrick, Barrett Lane**, is a 1991 infill project by Ottawa architect Barry Hobin and Charlesfort Development Corporation. Two bays feature wooden porches that integrate into the Lowertown streetscape.

Number **204–210 St. Patrick, Brousseau Terrace**, is decorated with dramatic cliffhanger porches. There is also the characteristic Lowertown carriageway to the rear of the lot. The flat-roofed terrace was built in 1898 by Evangeliste Brousseau as a Victorian two-storey investment property. The fancy brickwork patterning on the front somewhat alleviates its plain façade.

Continue west on St. Patrick. As you walk towards Parent you will see Notre-Dame's two spires. The rear view of the apse shows its splendid Gothic curves and buttresses. Turn right (north) down Parent Street and continue until you reach Bruyère Street. Turn left (west) at the corner of Parent and Bruyère. Built in 1916, **62 Bruyère** is a painted brick fourplex, with a central gabled parapet breaking its flat-top roof.

This large city block bounded by Bruyère (south), Dalhousie (east), Sussex (west) and Cathcart (north) shows the tremendous impact of the Grey Nuns upon Ottawa. The Nuns arrived in Bytown on February 20, 1845, and built their first hospital at 167 St. Patrick – a wooden frame building with dormers. Although it soon proved inadequate, the Order was thwarted for many years in its attempts to purchase more land and build a larger hospital. The typhus epidemic of 1847 helped convince reluctant politicians that the nun's petition was justified.

On the north side of Bruyère is the **Elisabeth Bruyère Health Care Centre**. It is a composite of buildings erected after Confederation – 1898, 1909, 1929, 1949 and 1953 – that reflects the forever-expanding needs of the capital's population. The east wing addition was designed by the firm of Noffke, Morin and Sylvester, erected upon the original site of the wooden typhus hospital. Noffke's plans can be viewed in the National Archives. They describe the layout for operating rooms, birthing rooms, private, semi-private and common wards.

Number **40 Bruyère**, opposite the hospital, is an early wooden clapboard Quebec-style house. Two dormer windows punctuate the roof. Note the offset doorway. A common later addition to these early dwellings was a rear kitchen extension built to alleviate the cramped living quarters. The original rear dormer windows were lost in the construction of these additions.

Continue along Bruyère to Sussex Drive. At the corner, look up to see the **sundial** designed in 1851 by the nun's geometry teacher, Father Jean-François Allard. It graces the 1849 Mother House of the Grey Nuns. A limestone wall, stabilized and repointed in 1992, encloses the front garden on Sussex.

Turn right (north) on Sussex Drive. On the southeast corner of Sussex and Cathcart is the old St. Joseph's orphanage of 1866. The two old stone buildings were connected by an addition in 1885. Cross Cathcart, and pass the now blocked-off end of Bolton Street, effectively barred to traffic. Proceed to Boteler Street and turn right (east).

You are now beside **255 Sussex**, the **Japanese Embassy**. Built in 1977, it was the first embassy in what the NCC calls Embassy Row. The wall was an integral part of the design by architect Takeshi Sakamaki with Murray & Murray, associate architects. It successfully juggles two functions: tight security and the enclosure of a graceful Japanese garden. The driveway leading through its walled confines is adorned with elegant sculpture, a tasteful touch repeated by ironwork at the entrance and on the ground floor windows. From its northeast (Boteler Street) side, look up to examine the embassy's layered planes, reflecting a design of simple massing.

After the older buildings of Lowertown, this embassy comes as an incongruous modern border to the parkland that is now the northern limits of this old neighbourhood. In the spirit of urban renewal and in an effort to create a ceremonial route from Parliament to Government House, the old streets and once bustling northern limits of Lowertown were razed. Landscaped lawns obliterate the memory of Redpath, Baird, MacKay and Carleton Streets. North of Cathcart were the tracks of the Bytown and Prescott Railway culminating in the MacTaggart Street station. In 1847–49 Irish squatters populated this area: imagine their rough-hewn houses dotted amongst the muddy, pot-holed roads and footpaths.

Now turn right on Boteler to **40 Boteler, Le Sussex**, the tall brick apartment building. Turn right (south) on Parent and walk to Bolton, then turn left, passing **163–165 Bolton**, the **Thomas O'Brien House**, an 1897 example of Lowertown's once common double residences. The four dormer windows in the bell-cast, mansard roof add extra light and space in the second floor. Many of the windows in these early structures were a combination of solid wooden shutters over oiled paper. Considering the rowdy reputation of Lowertown, they possibly served as useful protection, too.

Continue until you reach **Cathcart Square**, which was originally surveyed in 1846. It became an auxiliary market to Byward in 1877 on the recommendation of the City insurance inspector. Its proximity to the MacTaggart Street station allowed cattle to be brought to market, butchered and sold for retail to Bytown residents and for shipment to the lumber camps. Today there is nothing to remind us of the butcher's shops and meat stalls once crowding Cathcart Square. Instead, the quiet park is rimmed by neat end-gabled residences.

Turn right and cross the square. Continue south on Cumberland to Bruyère. On Cumberland notice the modern modular stone complex called **Oldentowne, 183–187 Cumberland**. Architect Barry Hobin's 1986 post-modern design imitates its historical Lowertown antecedents. Of special interest is its front façade with arched openings. It functions as a screen for roof terraces, affording residents privacy from the street. Look up behind this "false-front" screen to find the bracketed, pedimented parapet breaking the otherwise flat roofline. Dark, tunnel-like private entryways give residents privacy, but also pose a possible security problem.

Farther along is the heritage building **193 Cumberland**, **Rathier House**, built around 1862. This rough-cut stone building is a charming feature of the street. Built by carpenter Abraham Rathier as a combination residence and grocery shop, this classically-inspired house features a welcoming angled doorway. Notice the regularly spaced windows and the contrasting corner quoining.

Now walk left (east) on Bruyère to King Edward Avenue. The **Armand Pagé Community Centre** is on the corner, built in 1887 as Fire Station Number 5. This closed in 1952. The tower, which once served as a conveniently tall place to dry hoses (a characteristic feature of early fire stations), has long gone.

Cross King Edward at the traffic lights at St. Andrew. Walk back north to Cathcart and turn right (east). The 1981 **Cathcart Mews** complex of townhouses is now on your right as you walk towards the Rideau River. Like the Oldentowne complex on Cumberland, the Mews was built during the recent influx of middle class residents in to what was once the boisterous domain of squatters and raftsmen.

At the corner of Cathcart and Rose there is a park from which you can see the Rideau River. Just north of Cathcart, find the remnants of the old Bytown and Prescott Railway bridge, its stone supports still rising out of the river. Farther north you can see the Minto Bridges spanning the river between Green Island and New Edinburgh, to the east. Even in 1871, this was an isolated part of the city, the main reason for it being chosen for a hospital for infectious diseases.

*St. Anne's Church, an old Quebec tradition church.* NCC, M. Newton file H12-59, Box 54

Walk south along Rose, then turn left (east) on Bruyère. You pass the N.A. Bordeleau Park and, on the south side, **324–334 Bruyère**, flat-topped row houses, turn-of-the-century investment properties.

At the corner of Bruyère and St. Joseph, stop to observe the old brick duplex embraced by a new condominium complex which wraps itself around its host. Interestingly, the architect made no effort to integrate the old with the new: there is no common building material, no mirroring of red brick in the condominium. Instead, the California-style beige stucco walls boldly assert their newness. The stepped back floor plan cleverly affords privacy not only to ground floor entryways, but also to the roof terraces. These are further defined by stuccoed frames which add depth and movement to the streetscape. Now turn right on St. Joseph to view the less dramatic eastern façade of these row houses.

Turn left on St. Patrick Street. Behind a stone wall on your left are the gardens of **Good Shepherd Convent**, built in 1875. In 1961 The Ottawa Citizen called it "a convent for young ladies – formerly a home for wayward girls." Today it is the **Embassy of the People's Republic of China.**

Continue along the north side of St. Patrick until you reach traffic lights at Cobourg. On your left is the bridge leading to Island Lodge on Porter's Island. Cross the bridge for a brief glimpse of the grounds. The tall curved residence on the east side of the island, **Allan House**, was built in 1964 by McLean and MacPhadyen. The lower residence to the west is **Bradford House**. The rear of this building has a saw-tooth design, permitting maximum window space and delightful views of the garden and river. From the north side of the island you can catch a glimpse of New Edinburgh.

Backtrack across the bridge and cross St. Patrick Street at the lights to Cobourg Street. Turn right onto Old St. Patrick Street and walk the few steps west to **St. Anne's Church**.

This 1873 church, designed by architect J. P. LeCourt, is perhaps the only true example of the Quebec tradition of religious architecture in the city. It is characterized by a severely plain stone façade, allevi-ated by a medieval-inspired circular rose window, classical round-arched doors and statuary niches. The statues, side turrets and three entry doors balance each other both simply and beautifully. The effect is complemented by St. Anne's plain, three-tiered belfry.

Bishop Guigues was pivotal in the creation of St. Anne's parish. By the 1870s, Notre-Dame could not accommodate the booming Catholic population. The contractor who had built the Grey Nun's St. Joseph's

*St. Anne's Rectory. Nov. 1991.* K. Fletcher

Orphanage and General Hospital on Sussex, Pierre Rocque, teamed
with James O'Connor to assist architect J. P. LeCourt in building St.
Anne's. Guigues laid the cornerstone to the church on May 4, 1873.

   Take the footpath on the left (east) side of the church south to
Myrand Street. Here you will find **17 Myrand, St. Anne's Rectory**.
This is a 1921 W. E. Noffke design – in fact, it was the first of his many
Catholic commissions. Built in Noffke's much-loved Spanish Revival
style, this massive structure sports his favourite feature: a tiled roof.
But this building is by no means typical of Spanish Revival: its heavy-
looking form is peculiarly emphasized by large, smooth cut stone
blocks. Its classical two-storey portico with Corinthian capitals and a
pedimented door make this building an odd architectural hybrid.

   The rectory overlooks **Anglesea Square**, the second of the two
markets (the other being Cathcart) created in 1877 as additions to
Byward Market. Turn around, and with your back to the rectory look
at the Square: today's grassy playground echoes the bustling clamour
of bygone market days. Anglesea, however, had an even earlier use
as a rifle range. Yet it retained a "bad memory" for the community of
Lowertown East, when an unfortunate man was shot dead while
setting up targets one day. Eventually the rifle range was moved to
Strathcona Park (*see* Sandy Hill walk).

Playgrounds became necessities as urban populations grew. In his August 1903 report, Frederick Todd, OIC landscape architect, recommended "discontinuing the present road through the middle of the square and laying out the unimproved portion as a playground, with shade trees about the border and at a few other points." On May 5, 1913, the newly formed Playgrounds Association of Ottawa was granted permission to develop Anglesea Square as a children's playground.

Now look right (west) on Myrand towards the apartment on the western end of Anglesea Square. In the 1970s more than 300 houses in Lowertown West and East were demolished and 1,400 families were displaced. The multi-level and multi-coloured rows of townhouses and apartment buildings peppering the landscape represent the urban renewal projects undertaken jointly by the city, province and Canada Mortgage and Housing Corporation. It is to the credit of the people of Lowertown East that they have managed to maintain their largely French-speaking community centres in the face of the near annihilation of their neighbourhood.

Turn left on the walkway beside the apartment building at the foot of the playing field and walk south to York Street.

Number **340 York, St. Anne's School**, a typical "yellow brick box" school, sits at the end of York and serves the Catholic community of Lowertown East. Now turn right and walk west, returning towards the Byward Market area. On your immediate left is the "Collegiate Gothic" **310 York Street School**, designed in 1921 by architect William C. Beattie. Typical of this castle-like style are the stone-capped corner piers, complete with their slits for imaginary archers. Crenellated parapets and imposing Tudor-arched doorways are additional collegiate Gothic touches. Note the elaborately carved sign "GIRLS" over the east entry; its mate, "BOYS," is above the west portal.

Continue west on York Street and, as you walk, notice the all-too-rare unobstructed view of the Hill and the Parliamentary Library. Pass Nelson Street and note the original pressed tin exterior façade at **247 York**. Continue to King Edward.

On the corner is **321 King Edward**, the **Champagne Baths**. By the 1920s, city councillors were grappling with the concept of providing public recreational facilities for young and old alike. Many city dwellers could not afford the luxury of heading to the Gatineau Hills cottage country to escape summer's heat and dust. In a combined effort to promote health, recreation and "cleanliness among the poor," the Champagne Baths was built in 1922. The tiled roof is the signature of its architect, W. E. Noffke. (Its counterpart in the city is the Plant Bath in Plouffe Park, which opened at the same time at Gladstone and Preston. Although not designed by Noffke, this bath was also created by the City in a neighbourhood that, like Lowertown, lacked sufficient plumbing facilities.)

The front of the Champagne Baths is decorated, while the rear extension housing the pool is plain brick. On either side of the main entry are two smaller porch entries, accented by tiled caps. The main doorway is framed by double pilasters. Above it is an ornately curved broken pediment and window that carries the eye up to the wooden brackets supporting the overhanging eaves. The low-pitched roof was originally tiled with Noffke's favourites, today replaced by asphalt shingles. Unfortunately, clay tile cannot easily withstand the extremes of Ottawa's weather.

Cross King Edward at the lights and stop on the grassy median. It is here that the Bywash, the outflow of the Rideau Canal, curved from York Street to head north before connecting with the Rideau River. The boulevard was planned as a grand avenue to Rideau Hall, but the idea never caught on, despite the erection of the Minto Bridges connecting Lowertown to New Edinburgh via Green Island.

Looking left (south) from the median, you can see two other heritage structures. Number **351 King Edward** is **Ottawa Hydro**

*Ontario Hydro Sub Station #4. Oct. 1991.* K. Fletcher

**Electric Commission Substation #4**, designed in 1931 by the same William C. Beattie who designed the York Street School. This is an Art Deco building featuring a huge metal doorway that rises vertically to accommodate the transformer equipment. Note the copper canopy over the double front doorway attached by sturdy chains to copper rosettes. Copper panels and coping (flashing), sandstone and multi-paned windows animate this building's dark brick façade.

Farther south is the Moorish-looking **375 King Edward**, the **Jewish Memorial Funeral Chapel**, designed by J. W. H. Watts in 1904. A Star of David is prominently featured in the central window over the door and in the ironwork. Its front façade is extended by a curvilinear and stepped front gable, balanced on either side by onion-domed corner turrets.

At the turn of the century, Lowertown was an eminently desirable neighbourhood for many immigrants who wanted to establish businesses in the market area. Most built dwellings that had apartments above ground floor shops. Jewish immigrants started arriving in 1900 and started to build homes along Clarence Street. By 1930 they were the dominant ethnic group of the market business community and, to accommodate their special needs, kosher facilities were set up within the market building.

Now cross at the lights to the west side of King Edward. In early years, it looked quite different: once the Bywash coursed down here, flowing north from York Street up King Edward to the Rideau River. And, years ago, the boulevard was lined with gracious elms. Their loss from the Dutch elm disease in the 1950s and early 1960s devastated many streetscapes – this is no exception.

Continue walking west on York Street. On the right side of the street is **153–161 York**, the **Brown Tenements**. This is the only surviving example of a four-unit row in the area, and as such is a significant heritage building to remind us of what once were common, vernacular residences. Stand back to examine the façade and you will see the carriageway, now identified by a shabby wooden double door. Because the Brown Tenements extend the length of the lot allowance, a passageway was necessary to allow horse and wagon entry to the rear.

At the south corner is **350–352 Cumberland**, a pink brick double with gabled roof. It is a beautifully preserved home, which appears at first to be of classical proportions. But, in fact, its doors are asymmetrically placed, as are its two chimneys. One door is set at the extreme left end, diagonally balanced by the chimney at the far right;

the second entry is centrally situated just to the bottom right of the second central chimney. The six regularly spaced second-storey windows add to the overall illusion of symmetry. The brick veneer covers an earlier frame exterior.

Cross Cumberland to **126 York Street**, the **S. J. Major Building**. Sylvini Major and his wife, Marie Corinne Lebel, founded a grocery in the Byward Market. After his death in 1903, Mrs. Major and her son, Asconi Joseph, developed the business into the largest in Eastern Canada. In 1913, the family had a residence built in Rockcliffe at 541 Acacia. It is now known as Stornoway – home to the leader of the Opposition (*see* Rockcliffe walk). Their market business was merged in 1923 to form National Grocers. The S. J. Major building was a warehouse, but it is an attractive building nonetheless. Carved above the pedimented doorway are the words "S. J. Major Ltd." framed by two copper lions' heads. Extra interest is found in the rhythmic repetition of arches in the cornice and in the terracotta tiles relieving the brick façade.

Across the street is **113–115 York**, home to John Cundell, the last horse trader remaining in Ottawa. His spotless stable at the rear of the dwelling is home to the horses you still see hauling gaily painted wagons through Lowertown.

*Byward Market looking north to York Street. Note the wooden porches and frame buildings. Compare this bustling horse and carriage scene to the next photo. Both are taken from the same spot. NCC 172-4*

Continue west along York and cross Dalhousie at the lights. Number **325 Dalhousie**, on your left, is the **Union du Canada** building. Strong verticals and a bold capped roof are dramatically enlivened by slightly angled windows. Such uncommon window treatment creates intriguing reflection patterns – a feature that adds both texture and animation to the streetscape.

Number **62 York**, is the old **Richelieu Hotel**, today's **Stoney Monday's** bar and restaurant, named after the riot. Jean-Baptiste LaCroix leased the land from Colonel By in 1827. Ten years later, baker George Shouldice rented it as both a home and bakery until he purchased it in 1844. Shouldice built the present stone two-and-a-half storey building that became known as the Richelieu Hotel.

Continue west on York, and enter the **Byward Market** area. You see the **Byward Market Building** sandwiched between two one-way streets: William and Byward Market. Explore the lively market buildings and, in season, the open-air flower, vegetable, maple syrup and craft stalls. This Byward Market building is the fifth built in this Lowertown vicinity. All previous buildings were destroyed by fire.

The present building, built 1926–27 and altered in 1977 by the City of Ottawa Property Branch, has a functional design. It is essentially a long warehouse with a shed-like roof attached below the protruding

*Byward Market c1920: there is only one horse and wagon now, the mode of transportation has changed to the car. Frame buildings are now replaced with brick.* NCC 172-94

top storey, rather like a huge wrap-around verandah. It is well suited to shelter the outdoor stalls which enjoy its shade and shelter. Four cross-gables with their rounded-arched windows break the length of the structure which extends the length of an entire city block. The end gables also feature a round-arched window, and are further decorated by a contrasting flashing to the red brick and the black asphalt roof. Beneath the end gables find the seven square steel plates, which anchor the steel cables exposed in the interior of the roof.

Go inside the Market Building and walk upstairs to look down upon the craft stalls from the second-floor balcony. McClintock's Dream is the name of the papier maché sculpture by Victor Tolgesy which is suspended from the ceiling. The **SAW Gallery** is worth visiting at the southern end of the building.

The market's William Street façade is full of trendy restaurants, "country" shops and clothing stores. It is the Byward Market street façade that best approximates the ambiance of bygone market days. Sensitive heritage restoration by architect Julian Smith has restored many of the functional yet colourful buildings, featuring rounded-arch windows and polychromatic brickwork. Among these crowded cheese, meat, fish and poultry shops you can recapture the colourful Market days of old.

During summer, street buskers such as jugglers, street theatre groups and musicians compete with the bilingual calls of fruit and vegetable vendors. Bushel baskets overflowing with brilliant red and green peppers and long plaits of garlic compete for your interest.

To return to the start of the tour, head south on Byward or William to George. Turn right to the Ottawa School of Art.

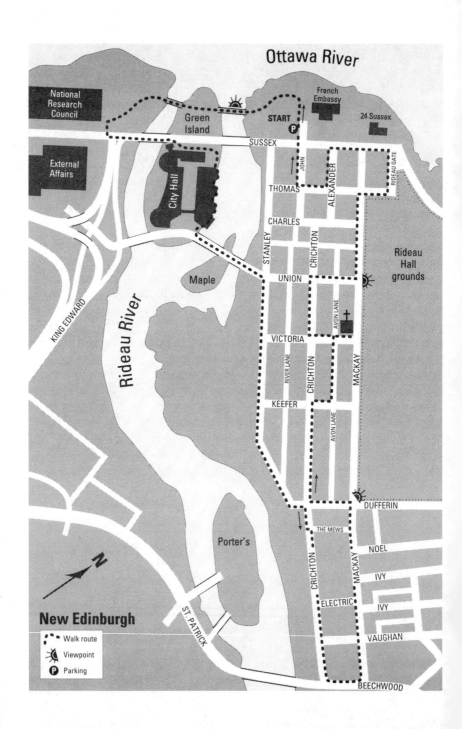

# New Edinburgh

## History

In 1613 French explorer Samuel de Champlain paddled past the curtain of the Rideau Falls and described its beauty in his journal. More than two hundred years later it was considered by Lord Dalhousie and Colonel John By as a site for the start of the Rideau Canal. It was bypassed in favour of Entrance Bay (*see* Parliament Hill walk). But Colonel By's canal contractor, Thomas MacKay, recognized the opportunity the falls represented. He purchased more than 1,100 acres of the surrounding land. In 1825 MacKay founded the village of New Edinburgh and encouraged his Scottish stonemasons and labourers to settle. He appears to have been a generous man, building homes for his labourers, donating land and labour for churches and schools.

*"Mill on the Rideau River, near Bytown," the present site of the National Research Council. Jean-Baptiste St-Louis' mill. W. H. Bartlett print. PAC-C-2368*

Today the parkland and municipal government buildings on Green Island belie the industry that once hugged the confluence of Rideau and Ottawa Rivers. The rattle of the horse-drawn street railway extending from New Edinburgh to the Chaudière and the whistle of the Bytown and Prescott train are both long gone. The "Mile of History," the once-dusty road connecting New Edinburgh's Rideau Hall to Ottawa is now busy Sussex Drive. Pigs and cattle no longer roam the streets to feed on the waste mash from Isaac McTaggart's 1840 distillery. His operation was located at the foot of Alexander Street which, in those early days, extended to the waterfront.

McTaggart's ale and whiskey was shipped by barge along the Ottawa River and Rideau Canal to its various destinations. The whiskey was piped downhill from the distillery into barrels. The distillery itself was driven by a thirty-five foot water wheel powered by water transported from the Rideau River via a three-foot wooden pipe.

The falls inspired Jean-Baptiste St-Louis to leave his mill at the Bywash on York Street, in Lowertown, to build the first mill at Rideau Falls in 1831. MacKay purchased it in 1837 and entered into partnership with several other businessmen including his son-in-law, John MacKinnon, resident of Earnscliffe. By 1847 their joint operation of a flour mill, cloth factory, distillery and saw mill was prospering on the west side of the falls. In one season the sawmill turned 20,000 Ottawa Valley logs into 2,400,000 board feet, most of it destined for the American market.

MacKay also built a cloth factory of stone, with "six looms, four double, two single, 150 yards of cloth per day and 25 employees."[8] By 1852 he owned and operated an extremely prosperous industrial complex at the Rideau Falls. The buildings were variously built of wood or stone. They included a large woollen factory where raw wool was carded and woven into fine tweeds, blankets and flannels; other mills produced shingles and doors, Venetian blinds and assorted farm equipment. As many as a hundred horse-drawn wagons could be seen along this part of Sussex, as farmers waited to stock up with much-needed provisions.

In 1851 MacKay received the gold prize from the London Exhibition for his New Edinburgh blankets. By the 1870s imported bales of wool from South America, Australia, England and the United States shared warehouse space with domestic raw wool.

After MacKay's death in 1855 the mills continued operation, eventually being purchased in 1866 by the Maclaren brothers of Wakefield

*MacKay Mills on east side of Rideau Falls, c1900 photo by Samuel J. Jarvis.* NCC, M. Newton files M12-004A&B, Box 41

and subsequently, in 1894, by the W. C. Edwards Lumber Company. In 1907 fire destroyed much of the original complex. Although the mills were rebuilt, they did not regain their dominance of the market. By this time the easily accessed Ottawa Valley pine and hardwood stands had been logged.

In 1928 the Dominion Bureau of Statistics purchased the mill complex on Green Island. One year later the National Research Council took over the mill buildings west of the Rideau and their 1930 annual report announced that the Edwards mills were to be the testing facilities for airplane engines. By 1943 the federal government owned the land extending from the site of the French Embassy to Earnscliffe. That year, the Edwards family, of lumbering fame, lost their protracted bid to retain their family home, now 24 Sussex Drive, the Prime Minister's residence. From 1956–59 the NCC demolished most of the old industrial complex surrounding Rideau Falls.

Contemporaneous with its industrial development was New Edinburgh's development as a working class residential neighbourhood. Properties along its western boundary at MacKay and Rideau Gate were coveted as they overlooked Government House. There, large homes are in stark contrast to the modest doubles, single family homes and apartment rows of clapboard, board and batten and brick that line the streets between Sussex and Beechwood.

Today the gentrification of the village is well underway. Population density is on the increase as infill destroys former gardens and multi-storey condominiums replace older structures. However, there are still many gems in this workers' village, and many a clue to its heritage still stands.

## Neighbourhood Styles

There is an agreeable mix of buildings in the village. The old stone schoolhouse that Thomas MacKay first built for his workmen and subsequently turned into a school for labourer's children still stands. A few frame homes survive, some clad in clapboard, and one or two in board and batten. There's an eclectic mix of rambling Victorian farmhouses of polychromatic brick and classically inspired stone residences. And, always dominating New Edinburgh is Rideau Hall, "MacKay's Castle." Its carefully nurtured "natural" landscape is circumscribed by a neat wrought iron fence with limestone pillars. Governors general hold levees twice yearly and there are tours of the grounds in the summer, giving visitors an opportunity to appreciate this stately oasis. However, even Rideau Hall's pastoral woods are now in jeopardy: Governor General Hnatishyn may receive permission to dig up some of the old woods to plant a rose garden.

Between Dufferin Street and Beechwood the neighbourhood mood changes. Here, the community of Lindenlea begins, and there are more commercial buildings, more flat-topped apartment blocks and, on Beechwood, the welcoming doors of cafés, book shops and variety stores.

## Walk Tips

5.5 km; 2.5 hours. Park your car in the lot at the foot of John Street, beside the French Embassy on Sussex Drive. Because most of the village is composed of private residences, not public buildings, there is little opportunity to explore interiors.

## The Walk

Follow the path heading west (left) at the north end of the parking lot, overlooking the Ottawa River. Continue until you reach the **Rideau Falls**, a tourist attraction since the earliest days of Bytown and the site of the city's early cloth and saw mills.

Cross the footbridge over the Rideau River to **Green Island**, so named after Patrick Green, who quarried stone for the canal. Green

*Mills on west side of Rideau Falls.* NCC, M. Newton file M12-004A&B

grew hay and pastured cattle on this twelve-acre island. By 1864 Muley's Saw Mill and Stave Factory had been built on the island, and, in Confederation year, on the north tip a foundry was opened which operated until 1922.

Cross the second footbridge to the west bank of the river and walk towards the **National Research Council, 100 Sussex**. Architects Sproatt and Rolph designed it in 1930–33, using the classical revival style popularized by the Parisian École des Beaux-Arts. Its monumental scale, massive columns and symmetrically balanced entrance pavilions declare solidity and importance. Prime Minister Mackenzie King personally selected the inscription about Truth carved above the doorway.

Cross Sussex Drive at the lights and head left (east) to view the **Ottawa City Hall** complex on Green Island. It is a juxtaposition of the old (1958) International Style city hall and Moshe Safdie's postmodernist 1992–93 creation which wraps around its predecessor and dominates Green Island.

Safdie's design is a composite of the geometric forms of cube, cylinder, triangle and circle. Walking east from Sussex, you first see its northwest entrance tower, a pyramidal structure within a cube. To balance this, the southwest corner of the Bytown Pavilion (its western wing) has a cylindrical block base with a cone-shaped glass roof. This houses Victoria Hall, the council chambers, which opened March 3, 1993. The pyramids of glass can best be appreciated if you enter the city hall: they bathe the interior atriums in welcome natural light.

Continuing east on Sussex, the International Style city hall now appears. It won the Massey Award of 1958 for architects Rother, Bland and Trudeau. Its repetitive rectangular design of glass, limestone cladding and aluminum is broken by the prominent three-storey mass over the main entrance. Safdie's city hall does not totally obscure the old: instead, its sheer, buff-coloured walls offset the grey International Style building.

Now turn right (south). Find the pathway along the east side of the island which follows the curves of the projecting "bubbles" of Safdie's Rideau Pavilion (the east wing). In the winter of 1992–93, the Rideau River overflowed its banks and froze right up to the base of the bubbles. Traditional spring blasting of the river keys to open up the flow was anticipated with concern.

As you emerge from the bubbles into the gardens at the rear of the city hall, you see the Unity Tower: it is not Safdie's original design, which was too expensive to complete. This open steel truss is merely the "innards" or frame of his concept, which included two elevators designed to transport visitors to a spectacular glass-covered, observation deck. In 1993 the mayor of Ottawa, Jacquelin Holzman, and the Board of Trade started a fundraising campaign to raise the extra $750,000 needed to complete the tower. Look to your right to appreciate the fountain and interior "courtyard" created between the two wings of Safdie's city hall.

Now turn left (east) to cross the **Minto Bridges**, built in 1900 by the Dominion Bridge Company of Montreal. Lady Minto encouraged the erection of these bridges as a possible ceremonial route linking Rideau Hall to Parliament via King Edward Avenue. As you cross the iron and steel span over the easternmost branch of the Rideau River, you enter the Village of New Edinburgh. Before leaving the bridges, note the stylized crowns adorning their spans.

Before turning right on Stanley Street, pause to look at **92 Stanley**, a picturesque stone cottage built in 1862 by J. Dougal MacLeod, a Scot from the Isle of Skye. MacLeod was a miller who worked in MacKay's Rideau Falls flour mill. The fine stone home has a wooden porch with a trellis motif.

Walk south on Stanley. Number **97 Stanley**, **Gerard House**, built in 1867 was the first home of William Gerard, who later moved

*92 Stanley.* NCC, M. Newton file H12-38, Box 44

because of the regular flooding of the Rideau River each spring. Each year, basements of homes up to Crichton Street were filled with water despite the dyke residents built to arrest the floodwaters. Until the City commenced the annual spring blasting and cutting of keys in the river ice the flooding continued. Even today basements throughout the city can get wet during spring runoff. Number 97 was originally a single family T-shaped dwelling, but it has been much altered over the years, and in 1949 Dr. R. E. Wodehouse converted it to a duplex.

Continue south to **110, 114** and **116 Stanley**, pretty wooden clapboard homes with well-preserved gingerbread (bargeboard) trim beneath their steeply gabled roofs. Number 114 was the first, built in 1865 by Henry Avery, master carpenter and cabinet maker for Thomas MacKay. He then built 110 for his son, Clinton, and then 116 in 1895 for his daughter, Margaret. A delightful picket fence defines one garden. In bygone days fences were a functional protection against

*151 Stanley, the Bell House. Oct. 1959.* C. C. J. Bond. NCC, M. Newton file
M12-004A&B

free-ranging cattle, horses, pigs and chickens, which otherwise
munched their way indiscriminately through lawns, vegetable plots
and flower beds.

Across from these houses is **119 Stanley**, the clapboard home of
John Jones, mill worker, built around 1892. Its cap-like mansard roof
is characteristic of Second Empire style, relatively uncommon here in
New Edinburgh. Farther south is **127 Stanley**, an example of unusual
exterior finishing in wood: vertical board and batten.

Continue south to **151 Stanley**, the **Bell House**, built in 1868 for
New Edinburgh physician Dr. W. R. Bell. *The Ottawa Citizen* of March
7, 1970 reported: "When Dr. Bell built the house on Stanley Avenue
… his offices were next door in the red brick row (then frame) with a
connecting passageway to the house. In about 1883, as the doctor's
family grew, a wing was added on the east side which explains the
rather odd shape of the house from the outside. Too, the house is now
in reverse from the original – the front door used to face the Rideau
River."

*St. John Evangelical Lutheran Church. Nov. 1991.* K. Fletcher

The Victorian detailing on this home includes polychromatic brick chimneys and alternating courses of scalloped and square shingle siding. Delicately carved dentil trim beneath the eaves of the porch roof and the turret-like dormer in its main roof add an airiness to the façade. The porch supports feature inset panels of crocketed lattice trim, which adds a light touch to the home. Look at the bargeboard or gingerbread trim: you can see different designs as additions were made to the original structure.

Turn left (east) at Dufferin and almost immediately right on Crichton. This street is named after Thomas MacKay's wife, Anne Crichton. The New Edinburgh streets John, Alexander, Thomas and Charles were named after just four of their children.

On the left (east) side of Crichton is **St. John Evangelical Lutheran Church**, a white clapboard church built in 1895 by August Bochner, who also built the parsonage in 1903. Bochner was one of the many Lutherans who settled in New Edinburgh after fleeing religious and political persecution in Germany. Pointed arched windows with diamond-shaped panes, and a steep gable roof adorned by a hipped bell tower with Gothic arched openings are its main features.

Farther down is **278 Crichton**, a still-beautiful 1908 Rogue Victorian brick home that is a study in competing shapes and forms. Its right side features a rounded tower two-and-a-half stories high. The bell-shaped dome is peaked with a rounded finial. The squared-off central doorway and the balcony alcove is a later addition built when the single family home was turned into the Philip Apartments by the Betcherman family in the 1930s.

As you continue south along Crichton, you will notice the streetscape is filled with increasingly high density buildings. The west side of the street is dominated by flat-top apartments. Flat-topped roofs became popular in the 1860s in Ottawa as they allow full use of the top storey, unlike the angled attic imposed by gabled roofs. Utilization of all available space was a desirable design feature when building apartments or business properties.

Numbers **309–321 Crichton** are flat-top units of wood frame construction with red brick veneer, sporting new copper cap canopies above each doorway. The flat roof is finished with a wood cornice. Note how the apartment block is built up to the sidewalk: there is no allowance for grass as the building itself takes up the entire lot.

Of similar construction, **323–337 Crichton** on the northwest corner at Beechwood features recessed doorways and porches, partitioned by tongue-and-groove curved wooden dividers for privacy. The cornice and porch entablature are painted pressed tin.

Contrast the streetscape of old apartments on the west side of Crichton with the brand new complex of post-modern brick units across the street.

*278 Crichton, the Rogue Victorian. Oct. 1991.* K. Fletcher

Turn left (east) on Beechwood and then left (north) again on MacKay. Note **25 Beechwood**, the 1990 **Royal Bank** building, a post-modern design by Alistair Ross and Associates. A precast concrete frieze depicting a crowd of people is set above the doorway, which is rounded at the corner. This is an inviting design feature, common to storefronts since the 1800s (*see* Lowertown walk, and Rathier House's angled entry).

The post-modern style makes clear reference to the historical precedents in commercial architecture. Here, the architects included

*Post-modern complex at 320 Crichton. Oct. 1991.* K. Fletcher

parapeted gables, a masonry stringcourse and a concrete cornice with end brackets. The mansard roof punctuated by dormers and a rusticated brick façade complete the historical references of the bank. Across from it on the south side of Beechwood, a brick post-modern mall continues the historical detailing.

Now turn left (north) on MacKay Street. Find numbers **339**, **341** and **343 MacKay**, a series of modern homes that feature sharply broken rooflines. This feature allows light to flood inside the homes through the windows that face this roofline. The three modern homes crowding the single lot have a distinctly different relationship to the street than do the heritage houses. Notice how they present a completely blank face to the street. Their design deliberately shields their residents from the community: thus the architecture isolates residents *from* rather than integrates them *into* their neighbourhood.

*Garvock House, featuring a turned wooden porch, contrasting quoins and twinned gables. Oct. 1959.* C. C. J. Bond. NCC, M. Newton file H12-48, Box 44

*58, 60 and 62 Crichton: board and batten, clapboard, and stucco finishing. Oct. 1991. K. Fletcher*

Farther along MacKay is **St. Luke's Evangelical Church**, built in 1915 at the corner of Noel. Known as Perpendicular Gothic, this style features a shallow "basket handle" arched doorway, with pointed arched panelling on its wooden door. The dark brick, square-steepled structure is well supported by prominent buttresses. Rectangular leaded paned windows set off by tracery add interest to this church, one of more than twenty Ontario Lutheran churches designed by architect W. E. Noffke.

At the corner of Dufferin is **MacKay United Church**, built in 1909 by New York architect H. F. Ballantyne. In 1874, led by Thomas MacKay's daughter Annie, local Presbyterians started a subscription for what became known as the New Edinburgh Presbyterian Church. The original rubble stone church was designed by Robert Surtees in 1875 for $5,000. Annie financed the building of the manse during the previous year.

From this corner you can see the wrought iron fence marking the limit of Rideau Hall. Turn left (west) on Dufferin and at Crichton head right (north) past **Crichton Street Public School**. The first two-room public school was built here in 1875, an addition in 1906, and a wing containing ten rooms built in 1919–20. The architect of the 1919 addition was William Garvock, but he died in December 1918. It was

W. C. Beattie, his successor, who supervised its construction. The flat-topped school is brick with an Indiana limestone trim and base.

Farther north find **139–141 Crichton, Garvock House**, a rare example of a once-common stone double residence. Ottawa once boasted many such stone doubles when canal stonemasons were building their own and rental housing. Its style is a mixture of Gothic, characterized by steep front gables, and classical features such as end gables with symmetrically placed chimneys. Stone brackets with a scroll design give sturdy roof support.

Turn right (east) on Keefer, named after MacKay's son-in-law and prominent Canadian engineer, Thomas Coltrin Keefer. Turn left (north) again to walk up Avon Lane. These lanes originally provided access for tradesmen delivering puncheons of water and coal by horse-drawn cart. A short walk down Avon Lane takes you to Victoria.

Before turning left (west), walk to your right to view the stone Anglican church of **St. Bartholomew**, affectionately called St. Bart's. Built in 1868, it was designed by Thomas S. Scott. St. Bart's is still a popular village church serving Lindenlea, New Edinburgh and Rockcliffe. Its steeply pitched, dominant roof and rough limestone walls lend St. Bart's a medieval aspect. This was deliberate. Both St. Alban's

*Rideau Hall with family of Viscount Monck, Canada's first governor general, posing for camera, 1868. Photo taken by Sam McLaughlin, commissioned by Sir John A. Macdonald.* PAC-C5966

(*see* Sandy Hill walk) and this church reflect the Anglican Church's reform movement, when a return to the old liturgy not only affected the service itself, but, symbolically, also Anglican architectural style.

St. Bart's has a colourful history. From its beginning, seats were free. Its solid stone walls lined with brick provided sturdy insulation, but the interior must have been chilly when heated with its original wood stove. Lord and Lady Dufferin were among the many governors general who attended the church. On Christmas Day, 1872, Lady Dufferin wrote in her journal: "Thermometer 10° below zero [Fahrenheit]. Proprieties out of the question – must go to church in sealskin turbans and must undress when we get there, as we sit near the stove, so that when we leave the amount of things to be put on is frightful."

Now backtrack and turn right (north) on Crichton. Numbers **58**, **60** and **62 Crichton** are lovingly restored frame cottages, complete with tidy gardens in front. Each boasts a verandah and pretty bargeboard beneath a Gothic Revival gabled roof. Front porches of various styles became popular in the mid 1800s, as a place to "take the air" and appreciate precious leisure time.

Number **48 Crichton** is a tiny stucco building with an intriguing garage that sports a pedimented parapet roofline with corner "battlements" and pressed tin siding. In bygone days, sashes and doors were

*Skating parties at Rideau Hall were extremely popular.* NCC, M. Newton file H12-052

made here. Farther along is **51 Crichton**, the **Tubman Home**, at the corner of Union. It is a rambling clapboard "farmhouse," with a large garden on a corner lot. The Tubman family lived here from 1874 until 1986.

On the northeast corner at Union is **42 Crichton, McCreery's**, which has been an important community grocery since 1902. Inside the shop you can see the original pressed-tin ceiling, and the wooden flooring and shelves. McCreery's is the sole store left in the village proper, and as such is an important heritage landmark.

Walk right on Union towards Rideau Hall's distinctive fence of pedimented stone pillars and wrought iron. Turn left (north) on MacKay. Here starts a row of distinctive homes of varying styles, from classical Georgian symmetry to whimsical Victorian Gothic built in the 1970s and 1880s. Each home has its special charm.

Number **87 MacKay, Maison Fréchette**, was the residence of Achille Fréchette, lawyer, and Annie Howells Fréchette, writer, journalist and friend of poets Duncan Campbell Scott and Archibald Lampman. The Fréchettes held evening soirées and readings here. This home is a good example of the Victorian's love for asymmetry. Look at the two flanking dormers: their windows are completely different shapes and sizes. Also, the front entry is offset. Now walk a few steps north and look back at the front door. There is an assortment of windows of various shapes: round, rectangular and arched, which are placed at staggered heights. The effect is one of movement and surprise – a far cry from the rigid precision of classical symmetry.

Number **73–75 MacKay** is a double Victorian Gothic red brick cottage. William Woodburn, a carpenter at MacKay's sawmill, built this home around 1874, and the whimsical wishbone bargeboard beneath its steeply peaked gables may have served as advertising for his woodworking skills. The picturesque design of this double, with its contrasting corner quoins, adds a romantic note to the streetscape. Symmetry is achieved by the twin front gables and emphasized by their crowning finials, the front porch and bay windows.

Number **55 MacKay** provides an interesting contrast. Although Victorian Gothic in feeling, this large house possesses many features associated with the Italianate style. Note the sturdy porch columns and pediment and, beneath the front gable, the three-panelled Palladian window, its central pane topped with the characteristic curved moulding. Victorian detailing abounds in the left-hand turret which has peaked dormer windows. Its height is surpassed by the ornate red brick chimney on the opposite side of the house. Built around

1898, the house was the residence of lumberman Gordon C. Edwards. Note the lovingly preserved carriage house to the rear of the home, with its cupola atop the gambrel roof.

At the corner of Thomas is **35 MacKay–71 Thomas**, a two-and-a-half storey, classically inspired house, built in 1864–65 for James Allen, a New Edinburgh merchant and, by 1867, the village tax collector. The house is also said to have been built by Anne MacKay, wife of Thomas, for white-collar mill employees.

Originally a single-family home, it was divided into two apartments in the 1870s. Classical features include the central doorway on MacKay, which is repeated in the side entry on Thomas. Both doors are framed by a rectangular transom above and sidelight windows which allow light into the hall. The roughcut limestone is softened by smooth corner quoins and lightened by the delicate bargeboard trim. The pedimented front porches were added in 1925 by tenant Allan Keefer, son of T. C. Keefer.

All of these homes on MacKay overlook the vice-regal estate. A close look at **1 Sussex Drive, Rideau Hall (Government House)**, itself is possible only if you go on one of the scheduled walks or attend a twice-yearly public levee. To glimpse the estate, turn right on Thomas Street, which becomes Rideau Gate. An octagonal gatehouse just inside the grounds was built at the time of Lord Monck's residency, in 1868.

The original Regency style country house was locally known as "MacKay's Castle," built in 1837–38 by Thomas MacKay. The estate was purchased by the federal government in 1868 for $82,000 as a vice-regal residence in perpetuity. A series of rambling additions commenced at that time which have almost completely obliterated the original design. However, if you go inside the grounds, look for the curved bay projecting from the rear of the southwest façade, part of MacKay's original building. In 1913 an immense royal coat of arms was added over the front doorway.

But Rideau Hall could and did inspire guests at dazzling vice-regal functions. Annie Howells Fréchette (whose house you just admired at 87 MacKay), catalogued the guests of Lord and Lady Lorne and itemized the entertainments, including dinner parties, balls, "at homes," skating and tobogganing parties, and theatricals between the years 1879 and 1881. By far the most popular were the latter events which saw 2,000 guests each year attend the winter sports parties and 1,300 a year the theatricals.[9]

Guests exclaimed in wonder at displays of fairy-lights illuminating the garden walks and thoroughly enjoyed participating in the rather more informal idiosyncrasies of their Excellencies. These included the fun-loving, albeit hazardous, way of lighting Rideau Hall's interior gas lamps. Lord and Lady Lorne's guest Victoria Sackville-West tells us how she lit them: "by rubbing [my] feet in the carpet all along the big corridor and putting my nose in contact, at the end, with the gas-burner."[10]

The approach to Rideau Hall is the short street called Rideau Gate, which is dominated by sedately classical homes. Number **7 Rideau Gate** was built in 1867 and is, since 1966, the official guest house of the Government of Canada. It is a solid Georgian-inspired home ideally situated between Rideau Hall and 24 Sussex.

Number **5 Rideau Gate, Edgewood**, now the **Embassy of South Africa**, was once the home of "Minto's Folly," the charming Lola Powell, mistress to Governor General Lord Minto in the heady young years of this century. The second storey of Edgewood is an addition to the original 1841 home. You can easily discern the joinery in the stonework between the addition and the original structure. This is yet another house touched by the architectural hand of W. E. Noffke, whose May 14, 1947, plans note the addition of "galvanized iron coping and imitation stone to match existing [stone]," and a specification to include a "galvanized iron band [exterior stringcourse] to match existing."

Before heading west on Sussex, look at **24 Sussex Drive**, the Prime Minister of Canada's residence, named **Gorffwysfa**, Welsh for "a place of peace." The original 1867–68 Gothic villa with a central doorway framed by an overhead gable, built for mill owner Joseph M. Currier, has long vanished, victim to a succession of alterations by the Department of Public Works (DPW). In 1943, Emmet P. Murphy of DPW recommended federal purchase of the property to prevent further commercial development of the river frontage. In 1950, after years of renovations, the house was offered to Prime Minister Louis St. Laurent as official residence. He always preferred his rented apartment in the Roxborough Apartments.

At the time of expropriation, DPW had no plans for the home, which lay vacant for over a year. In November 29, 1949, architect Gustav Brault thought repairs totaling $168,000 were adequate. As work progressed, Brault's figure rose to $410,000.

*34 Alexander, Henderson House, with its beautiful wishbone gables. Oct. 1959.*
C. C. J. Bond. NCC, M. Newton file, Box 44

The interior was completely gutted: carved wooden panelling and a gently curving ten-foot-wide oak staircase were ripped out. The exterior suffered: gone is the original Gothic gabled home with its prominent oriel window, replaced by a sprawling house of rambling style. Successive prime ministers have added their own touches, including a swimming pool in 1975 during the tenure of Pierre Elliott Trudeau. Both this house and Stornoway, the leader of the Opposition's official residence in Rockcliffe, are routinely redecorated at public expense each time new residents move in.

Continue west on Sussex, on the south side of the street, then turn left (south) on Alexander. On your right is the remnant of a stone wall built by Isaac McTaggart that once supported a glass hothouse.

At the corner of Thomas stop to look at **34 Alexander, Henderson House**, built for John Henderson, manager of the Maclaren lumber company. This Second Empire design features fanciful wishbone gables on all four sides of its otherwise mansard roof. Notice the round-headed windows below the fire escape on the north side. These are echoed by the rounded pediment over the doorway. The home was originally painted white with black roof, porch and trim, which proudly emphasized its design elements. Duotone colour schemes were extremely popular at the turn of the twentieth century; black and white providing the most dramatic contrast.

The square section on the west side of the house was originally the conservatory. But in 1937 the home was turned into apartments and the plant collection moved to Rideau Hall. Once famed for its beautiful gardens, today this house is victim of infill and additions. Henderson House is now cramped on a lot too small for its scale. Gentrification of the village has its drawbacks.

Turn right (west) at Thomas and right again on John Street. Walk due north to cross Sussex to your car. On your right you pass **62–64 John**, built in 1837 by Thomas MacKay as a home for his millworkers. He later converted it to a schoolhouse where Montreal teacher James Fraser taught the three Rs. In 1848 the building reverted to rental premises. By the 1960s, the NCC had plans for the river waterfront and the northern limits of New Edinburgh, and 62–64 John was expropriated, but saved from demolition by public outcry.

The classically symmetrical limestone stone exterior remains. But the NCC made many alterations in 1967: dormer windows and a rear extension were removed, a new shingle roof, modern doors and windows were added and the interior gutted.

*Rideau Falls showing extent of MacKay's Mill complex to east. Photo predates the 1958 International style city hall.* NCC, M. Newton file M12-004

Walk to Sussex. On your right is a plaque to the memory of Thomas MacKay, founder of New Edinburgh. Cross Sussex to find your car beside **42 John Street**, the granite **French Embassy**, which stands on the site of Isaac McTaggart's distillery. Built in 1936–39 by France's then chief architect of civil buildings, Eugène Beaudoin, it is the first embassy in Ottawa that was specifically built for that purpose. Note its dramatic, boldly framed windows.

MacKay and Burritt's sprawling mills have gone, as has McTaggart's distillery, but the new parkland has restored the beauty of Rideau Falls. Today, New Edinburgh blends old with new, struggling to retain its village texture. Gone forever, however, are some village memories. In his recollections of earlier times, former resident John Askwith wrote: "In those days the people of the Village could hear on a wintry night, the howling of the wolves which were concentrated between the East end of the present St. Patrick Bridge and the cemeteries. They came frequently on the winter nights."[11]

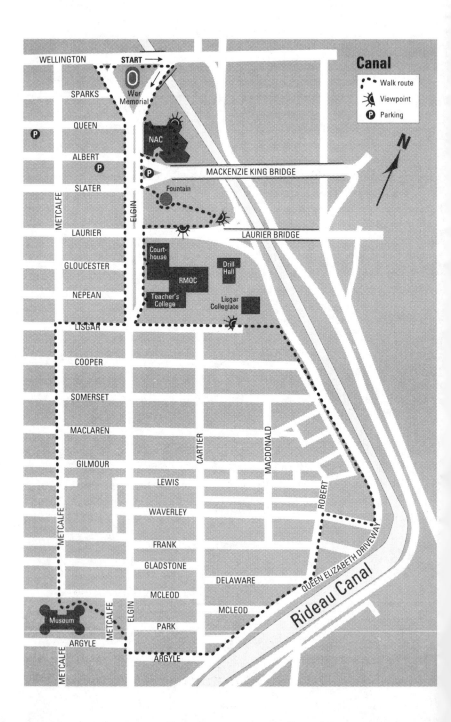

**Canal**

Walk route
Viewpoint
P Parking

N

WELLINGTON
START →
War Memorial
SPARKS
QUEEN
NAC
ALBERT
MACKENZIE KING BRIDGE
SLATER
Fountain
METCALFE
ELGIN
LAURIER
LAURIER BRIDGE
Court-house
GLOUCESTER
Drill Hall
RMOC
NEPEAN
Teacher's College
Lisgar Collegiate
LISGAR
COOPER
SOMERSET
MACLAREN
CARTIER
MACDONALD
GILMOUR
LEWIS
WAVERLEY
ROBERT
FRANK
GLADSTONE
DELAWARE
QUEEN ELIZABETH DRIVEWAY
MCLEOD
METCALFE
MCLEOD
Museum
ELGIN
PARK
METCALFE
ARGYLE
ARGYLE

Rideau Canal

# Canal

## History

This Ottawa neighbourhood began its life in 1827 as Corkstown, located on either side of the Deep Cut. The Deep Cut is the straight stretch of the Rideau Canal alongside the Drill Hall and Lisgar Collegiate, extending to Waverley (*see* map). Deposits of highly unstable leda clay caused the canal walls to repeatedly collapse, and the workmen had much difficulty digging the canal here. Because of this, excavations had to be especially deep and well stabilized: hence the name "Deep Cut."

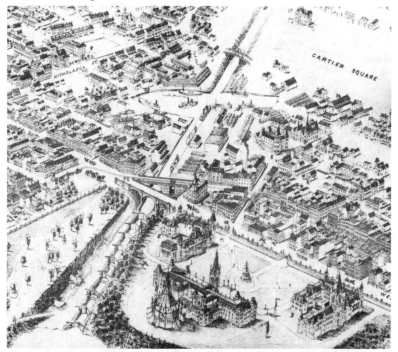

*Detail of 1876 map "Birds Eye View of the City of Ottawa" by Herman Brosius. Note the Canal Basin with several steamers at its docks. The Laurier Avenue Bridge was then just a wooden structure. NCC 172-301*

During the canal construction, Colonel By hired more than 300 Irish labourers. All needed housing but Bytown couldn't meet all their, and their families', needs at once. In 1827 Lowertown was still a cedar swamp. A large, mosquito-infested beaver meadow existed where Union Station now stands. Many Irish labourers hewed their own rough log shanties out of the dense woods to create Corkstown, so called, some say, not because they came from Cork in Ireland, but because of all the whiskey corks popping from eagerly consumed bottles. Other settlers squatted in hastily built wooden shacks in Lowertown after the Bywash started to drain its low, wet land. After the Vesting Act of 1844, when the Ordnance relaxed its control of Lowertown, most labourers moved there from Corkstown.

It was here in Corkstown that Mother McGinty's popular tavern kept the whiskey, beer and a cordial known as "shrub" flowing. It seems she ruled her whitewashed log watering hole with a kindly but iron hand. Mrs. McGinty kept track of credit by making a short mark on a blackboard for half pints, a long mark for a gallon – and collected with a judicious blend of good humour and what one poet called "the athletic charms ... of her bare arms."

Where Union Station and the National Arts Centre now stand was once the Canal Basin. The indented sides of the turning basin are filled in, but in early days there were landing docks for the steamers

The Rideau Queen *heading north towards the canal turning basin c1908. Note the original Parliament Centre Block on the upper left.* NCC 712-284

delivering or receiving freight and goods from the crowd of wooden warehouses lining the canal. The traffic was so busy that the wooden boards of the docks needed continual maintenance and repair. On either side of the Canal Basin, steamers jostled for a berth. Boats such as the *Olive, Rideau Queen* and *Pumper* docked here. And not all cargo was freight. Passenger traffic formed a respectable proportion of the canal trade. In the days before good roads or railways, water transportation was the way to go. Accordingly, steamers were outfitted with overnight berths for passengers travelling between Kingston and Ottawa – and beyond to Montreal.

The advent of rail effectively killed Rideau Canal water traffic. Government control of the Canal Reserve – the strip of land bordering the banks of the canal – was eventually relinquished. (Colonel By had reserved the lands in case they were needed for military fortifications.) The twin docks and turnaround areas of the basin were filled in. In 1910 the Grand Trunk Railway was ceded land on the east side of the basin, and in 1912 Union Station was built. The last passenger steamer, the *Ottawan*, left its capital wharf on November 2, 1935, thus ending a century-long chapter in Ottawa's history.

Government control of lands was a constant issue. Nicholas Sparks (after whom Sparks Street is named), an early Bytown resident, purchased 200 acres of land bordered by Wellington, Bronson, Waller and Laurier. When the present site of the Rideau Canal was finally selected by Colonel By in 1826, the Crown thwarted Sparks' intended development of his eastern properties. Eighty-eight acres between Elgin and Bank were seized for possible military defence, which prevented Sparks from extending his street to Elgin. A long dispute ensued that was finally resolved in 1845. Never one to waste time, Sparks immediately divided his land into lots and sold them. But it took years for this section of town to rival and then supersede the dominance of Sussex and Rideau as the business core of the capital. In the 1860s Sparks Street was gaining prominence, and by the 1880s brick and stone buildings sprang up, reflecting the confidence of entrepreneurs in this new business, professional and political centre of Ottawa.

As military threats died down after the Imperial troops left Ottawa in 1870, increasing pressure was placed upon the Crown to free up the Canal Reserve lands.

In 1832 By had purchased 600 acres for £1,200: today the property would be bounded by the canal, Laurier, Bronson and Gladstone Streets. In 1876 three well-known Ottawan entrepreneurs – James

*Russell House Hotel, corner of Sparks and Elgin. Oscar Wilde once stayed here.*
S. J. Jarvis. NCC, M. Newton file, Box 39

Maclaren, Robert Blackburn and Charles McGee – bought part of his estate. The three investors started the Ottawa Freehold Association in 1883 and the development of the area into mixed commercial and residential quarters began in earnest. Increasingly, commercial buildings of the 1880s were built with permanence in mind. Buildings with brick load-bearing walls, wooden floor frames and a stone or brick exterior finish started to spring up. Styles such as Italianate, (the Scottish Ontario Chambers) Queen Anne (the Central Chambers) and Second Empire (the Langevin Block) competed for attention along the Elgin Street façade.

In earlier days, the Elgin-Sparks corner was dominated by the Russell House. It started life in 1845 as the Campbell House, a three-storey, tin-roofed inn. As Ottawa grew, so did the hotel's fortunes. In 1863 it became the Russell House, a popular meeting place for politicians, lobbyists and journalists to argue and entertain one another with the latest gossip from the Hill.

The Russell's demise shocked residents. Its front doors were padlocked at 1:30 p.m. on October 1, 1925. It was destined to be demolished and make way for the creation of Confederation Square. While politicians and planners hummed and hawed, two and a half years passed. During the night of April 14, 1928, a flicker of flame was seen in the old hotel: the Russell was doomed. For three months its blackened hulk haunted the streetscape it had once graced. Then the wrecking balls tore it apart in July 1928. In the 1930s, Confederation Square took shape.

In 1899, Sir Wilfrid Laurier's Liberal government approved the creation of the Ottawa Improvement Commission. Its mandate was to plan the beautification of the capital. Frederick Todd's capital planning report of 1903 called for the effective landscaping of the industrial eyesore framing the Rideau Canal. His words are still appropriate today: "Careful study of natural scenery, or of good landscape paintings, will show how important is the arrangement of trees and shrubs. Few people realize that the same elements which combine to produce a beautiful landscape may also produce a landscape flat and uninteresting."

Metcalfe Street was promoted by several governments and individuals as a ceremonial route to the Parliament Buildings. Framed by beautiful elm trees, gracious residences and anchored by the splendid Victoria Memorial Museum (today's Museum of Nature), it seemed a regal approach to Canada's seat of power. Because the land immediately south of the Hill was already built up by 1867, the costs of expropriation, demolition and reconstruction were never approved.

*Rideau Canal, 1904, looking north towards present site of Union Station.*
NCC 172-141

Finally, in 1939 Jacques Gréber proposed changes to the ceremonial route: but it was not until 1951, when his Master Plan was accepted by Louis St. Laurent's government, that his changes such as the oblique approach to the Parliament Buildings via Elgin Street were adopted. The dream of Metcalfe as a grand approach to Parliament was dead.

## Neighbourhood Styles

The engineering marvel of Colonel John By's Rideau Canal lends visual continuity to this exploration of Ottawa. But many buildings of significance compete for attention. The National War Memorial provides a stunning start to the walk. Elgin Street – widened as far as Lisgar – boasts the colourful Italianate Scottish Ontario Chambers on the corner of Sparks Street Mall and Elgin, the Bell Block and the Central Chambers, all Ottawa heritage gems. However, in 1993 architects Brisbin, Brock and Benyan started a massive downtown development project to incorporate all three into a modern office complex for Perez Commercial Corporation and the Standard Life Assurance Limited. In the winter of 1993, the 1867 Bell Block was reduced to a thin, forlorn-looking façade wrapped in polyethylene to protect it from winter storms.

The old limestone Teachers' College opposite the former residence of well-loved physician Dr. James Grant, now Friday's Restaurant, provides yet another important link to Ottawa's past. And, architect David Ewart's Victoria Memorial Museum, now the Museum of Nature, is like a castle at the southernmost reach of this walk, deep in the heart of what was once Stewarton. The return route up Metcalfe Street evokes memories of past grandeur as you pass by the once-gracious mansions of Thomas Birkett and J. R. Booth.

The Canal-Metcalfe loop links symbols of national pride with seats of learning, private residences and commercial buildings. Tying it all together is the lovely parkland bordering the canal. The ring of picks and shovels have gone, as has the whitewashed tavern operated by well-loved Mrs. McGinty. Instead, paths through lawns and flower-beds lure the walker.

## Walk Tips

5 km; 2.5 hours.

You will be walking among parks, public buildings and private residences. Feel free to explore the interior spaces of the National Arts Centre, the Ottawa Courthouse and the Teachers' College, just to name a few of the public buildings on this walk. On Elgin Street you will find restaurants and shops to browse. As a special tip, it is well worthwhile visiting the War Memorial on November 11, Remembrance Day. Then, amid the crowds, the swirl of the kilts and the skirl of the bagpipes, Vernon March's sculpture takes on a life and symbolism of its own. (Note: in the description of this walk, the Queen Elizabeth Driveway has been abbreviated to "the Driveway.")

## The Walk

Start at the **National War Memorial** at the top of Elgin Street, southeast of Parliament Hill. Many buses arrive at this central location. If you are driving, find a parking space and make your way to the memorial.

The National War Memorial commemorates those who fought and died in World War I, World War II and the Korean War. The allegorical figures perched on top of the monument are winged Victory, and Liberty, who is holding a torch. Their flowing robes are reminiscent of the fluid, organic forms of the Art Nouveau period, and contrast markedly with the massive Beaux-Arts style granite base. Through the arch of the granite, soldiers and horses look straight down Elgin Street. Notice the different races represented among these realistically detailed soldiers. A symbol of the pride and hope of a young Canada, the memorial dominates Elgin's busy streetscape. British sculptor Vernon March died before finishing his work. Completed by his brothers and sister, the sculpture was unveiled by King George VI on May 21, 1939.

Walk around the memorial and cross Elgin at its northeast side. Turn right to walk south on the east side of Elgin. To your left is the dark brown, gracefully Brutalist **National Arts Centre**, built 1964–69 by the architectural team of Affleck, Desbarats, Dimakopoulos, Lebensold and Sise. Find the staircase leading up to the patios overlooking the canal. From here you can see the combination of hexagonal forms that describe the structure. Designed as a series of stepped terraces, which alleviate and animate its sheer walls, the building successfully integrates into its embankment overlooking the canal.

*National Arts Centre, "the most mysterious building in town" because no one can tell where the entrance is, according to architect Moshe Safdie.* NCC 186-94

Its elevation affords an unexpected perspective on **Confederation Square** – and you can catch a glimpse of the Gatineau Hills to the north. While facing north you will see old Union Station (*see* Sussex walk). Keep to your right to walk to the south side, from where you can see the picturesque Drill Hall fronting Cartier Square. Note the dominating form of the Ottawa Courthouse standing on the corner of Laurier and Elgin, beyond Confederation Park. From this perspective, note the courthouse's modern equivalent of towers, topped with squared-off caps slightly reminiscent of châteauesque detailing.

Find the stairs by the sculpture on the south façade of the Arts Centre. Walk down and turn right to return to Elgin Street. Turn left (south) and cross Albert and Slater Streets. These two streets merge on your left to cross over the canal: this is the Mackenzie King Bridge. Turn left again at the angled pathway into **Confederation Park**, which was created in the 1960s by a series of expropriations and demolitions courtesy of the NCC. Among the demolished buildings was the eighty-two-suite Roxborough Apartments, a popular hotel-apartment for many politicians, including Mackenzie King. This site was not intended as a park: the buildings were demolished to make way for the Museum of Natural Science. However, after life as a parking lot for years, the site was landscaped to create this popular park. Beneath its grass is a parking lot servicing the National Arts Centre.

The centerpiece of the park is a cascading fountain once located in Trafalgar Square, London. Surrounding it – and dotted throughout the park – are many commemorative sculptures and artworks. Angle through the park, keeping to your left until you reach the **Laurier Avenue Bridge**. Originally built of wood in 1872, when Laurier was known as Maria Street, the bridge provided a link to Sandy Hill and Lowertown. In 1900 a masonry and steel bridge replaced the original wood, and in 1943 the bridge was expanded again. In a spirit of heritage enthusiasm, the City has painted the turn-of-the-century spans green.

Now leave the bridge behind you. Walk west on Laurier Street, returning to Elgin. On your left you will pass the 1879 **Cartier Square Drill Hall**, a vernacular hybrid, which incorporates touches of Italianate and Second Empire details. Its polychromatic façade is Italianate, as are its multiple round-arched windows and stringcourse. Yet a Second Empire feeling is imparted by its centre raised parapeted gable and flanking corner pavilions which are topped with mansard caps. Apart from the addition of a new roof in 1981, the building is basically unchanged. During the devastating Ottawa fire of 1900 it provided refuge for many destitute and terrified families.

West of the Drill Hall is the Regional Municipality of Ottawa Carleton complex you will visit later on this walk.

You are now walking beside the 1986 **Ottawa Courthouse**. Architects Murray & Murray designed this severely Brutalist structure. The sheer walls of its imposing, almost windowless exterior feature fiberglass "boulders" projecting from its Elgin Street façade. It is a dominating presence that demands attention and respect – and which also imparts faceless anonymity.

Enter off Elgin to go inside the courthouse. Its interior space reflects an inward-looking design. There are busy offices, oak-panelled court rooms and public concourses. It is surprisingly light and airy, with a triangular-shaped central atrium that vertically connects all floors.

On your way out, on the first floor, locate Courtroom 24. Opposite, on the wall, is artist Jamelie Hassan's 1986 ceramic replica of Lieutenant Colonel By's 1830 map of the Rideau Waterway, "Water Communication." Hassan preserved By's original spelling of landmarks such as the "Gatteno" River and the Township of "Nipean."

*The Ottawa Courthouse, Nov. 1991. Its massive form dominates the corner of Laurier and Elgin.* K. Fletcher

Return to Elgin Street, turn left and find the **Ottawa-Carleton Centre**, the old **Ottawa Teachers' College**. Originally called the Normal School, it opened in 1875 at a cost of $81,000, as one of the first of three such schools in Ontario. Architecturally eclectic, the cut limestone building is a mix of styles: Gothic, Second Empire and Norman Romanesque. Second Empire is reflected in the building's overall massing, best evidenced in its Elgin façade. Note its central, mansard-roofed entrance pavilion. The doorway itself features a heavy looking rounded archway. Arched windows and colonnettes (small non-structural columns) are symmetrically positioned on either side of the door. Victorian Gothic touches such as the steep front gable with a trefoil motif, and steep-roofed belfries with pointed-arch openings add extra interest to this stylistic hybrid. In contrast to the post-modernist and Brutalist edifices along Elgin Street, this all-too-rare stone heritage building adds a humanizing touch to the streetscape.

If it is open, enter the Teachers' College to see its high and pattern-ed pressed-tin ceilings, the Victorian scrolled and panelled detailing of the staircase at the rear east end, and the deeply inset window ledges which indicate the thickness of its old stone walls.

Return outside to Elgin Street and turn left (east) on Lisgar.

To your left is the **Model School** attached to the rear of the Teachers' College. It opened for classes in September 1880, and operated for thirty years allowing teachers-in-training a "model" school in which to practice their professional skills prior to graduation. Built of cut, rough-surfaced stone, it is similar to the Teacher's College in its stylistic mix. When it opened, there were six class-rooms, an assembly room, a room for the head teacher, and a "recreation yard" more than 200 feet long.

Farther along Lisgar, and attached to the Model School, is **111 Lisgar**, the **Regional Municipality of Ottawa-Carleton** (RMOC) complex you saw earlier. Completed in 1990 to a cost of $87 million, architect Raymond Moriyama here designed a post-modern building complete with steel lattice bell-tower and sheer curtain walls. Go inside to view the council chamber. Its muted colours are in stark contrast to the hard surfaces of highly polished marble that dominate the RMOC's interior public spaces.

Keep left on Lisgar to **Lisgar Collegiate**, originally built in 1874 in the Gothic revival style by architects W. T. Thomas and W. Chesterton. At first, the buildings were poorly heated, and students and teachers alike often sat huddled in their coats to keep warm. The problem was rectified in 1888 when a heating and ventilation system was installed. By 1890, the school was seriously overcrowded. In 1892 James Mather designed an addition, but on January 30, 1893, the entire building burned. By mid-March, Mather had redesigned a completely new structure.

Like the original, the new building was faced in stone from Robert Skead's quarry in Nepean. Walk down the pathway on the school's west side to look at the projecting oriel window – the second-storey bay – on the north façade. As the student population continued to grow, so did the demands for additions: the years 1903, 1908, 1951 and 1962 all saw further construction designed by a number of architects. Return to the front of the building. The 1951 gymnasium by John Albert Ewart and A. J. Hazelgrove is connected to the front of the main building on Lisgar by an underground tunnel.

There are many scholastic motifs in the exterior carvings, including a set of books, a scroll and the symbolic oil lamp of learning, whose motif is also found on the University of Ottawa's Simard Hall on Waller Street (*see* Sandy Hill walk).

Before heading on to the Queen Elizabeth Driveway ("the Driveway"), look west along Lisgar to appreciate the integration of 1870s' and 1990s' architecture. Lisgar Collegiate and the Teachers' College share the skyline with the vertical striping of Place Bell Canada and the post-modern glass-and-brick Barrister House.

*Lisgar Collegiate. Nov. 1991.* K. Fletcher

Now walk towards the canal. Cross the **Driveway**, built 1900–05 by the Ottawa Improvement Commission. Head south along its landscaped embankments. You will also see two "modern heritage" landmarks on the opposite side of the canal. One is the stylized cross of the University of Ottawa tower; the second is the op-art eyes on McDonald Hall, the physics and computer science building.

When it was first built, the Driveway was narrower. Travelling along it by horse and carriage allowed time to view the ornamental gardens that originally featured formal arrangements. Automobile traffic dramatically altered the landscaping. Streets were widened. Flower arrangements became less formal because people couldn't appreciate the workmanship as they sped past. After World War II the designs changed again thanks to the annual donation of thousands of tulips by Holland, a tradition still upheld today, and a source of national pride.

At the southwest curve cross the Driveway and walk west on Waverley to Robert Street.

Architect Peter Pivko designed **53–55 Robert** (1988), a dramatic post-modern rectangle on the corner of Robert and Waverley. Sheer white stucco exterior walls are relieved with angled teal blue and magenta windows. Much to the alarm of some neighbours (who tried to prevent this house from being built), this surprising residence wakes up the neighbourhood with its "factory-like" appearance in a

*53–55 Robert. Oct. 1991.* K. Fletcher

sea of red-brick. The front is angled on its lot because of the imposed constraint of the property line itself, which is not square. Position yourself so you can look sideways along its façade to fully appreciate its windows which project at angles from the otherwise smooth frontal plane. (This contemporary, *post*-modernist home provides a fascinating comparison to the two modernist homes in Sandy Hill, on Goulburn and Range Roads.)

Turn left on Robert. On the right note the Rogue Victorian home, **65 Robert**. A fatly rounded, bell-capped turret adorns this red block residence with its asymmetrical, squared-off entryway, a sad later addition built when the single family home was turned into apartments. Unfortunately, this addition totally destroys the dignity of this otherwise beautiful home. (Its mate is 278 Crichton Street – *see* New Edinburgh walk.)

Turn right (south) onto the Driveway. On your immediate right is the Spanish Colonial Revival **Hungarian Embassy, 7 Delaware**. Prior to 1992, when its exterior walls were redone in honey-beige stucco, this house was painted a stunning – and surprising – robin's egg blue. With its beautiful diamond-shaped leaded glass windows and red Spanish tile roof, this 1900 residence was remodeled by W. E. Noffke in 1922. Note the curvilinear gable and the sweep of the flared piers

*7 Delaware, the Hungarian Embassy. Oct. 1991.* K. Fletcher

supporting the tiled, hip-roofed porch. Although crowded on a lot too small for its mass, the home adds charm and whimsy to the street.

Turn right (south) to walk on the paved path nestled between the back gardens of homes and a protective band of shrubbery lining the Driveway. On your right is **102–108 Driveway**, at the corner of McLeod. Beautifully curved two-storey porches and flanking Palladian windows give this angled, flat-topped co-operative its charm. Continue south until you reach Argyle Street.

Turn right (west) on Argyle and walk to Elgin Street. Cross at the lights and turn right again. On your left is the concrete and glass-bricked police station, **424 Elgin**. Its sloped glass roof facing the street is attractive but can be a menace in winter when snow and ice cascade onto the front entry. Every winter, barricades are erected to guide people safely inside.

The next block is the park grounds of the **Museum of Nature**, formerly the **Victoria Memorial Museum**. The museum was built for $1,250,000 between the years 1905 and 1912 by architect David Ewart. The builder, George Goodwin, employed 300 master stonemasons and stonecutters especially hired from Scotland. Walk around its magnificently ornate, castle-like exterior to view the detailed carvings and stained-glass windows. These windows are best seen

*The Museum of Nature: David Ewart's "castle". Nov. 1991.* K. Fletcher

from the interior: go inside, look up and appreciate their exquisite detail. They are highly reminiscent of the style of the Arts and Crafts Movement, having the feel of a William Morris design.

Ewart deliberately designed the museum as a balance to the Parliament Buildings in the days when Metcalfe Street was envisioned as a ceremonial route to the Hill. But, from the beginning, construction was fraught with complications. Because of unstable leda clay the foundations settled, and in 1915 the central tower started to pull away from the front of the building. The unstable clay forced Ewart to alter his original designs – an example, like St. Alban's in Sandy Hill and the Parliament Buildings, of the natural environment's influence upon style. Workmen were affected, too. Some threw down their tools, refusing to work in the basement as shifting foundations shot bricks and stones at them.

The museum has served various functions. After the February 1916 fire destroyed the Centre Block of Parliament, the Senate and House of Commons convened here until 1920, when it reverted to its former function as home to the National Gallery and the Geological Survey of Canada. In 1919 the state funeral procession of Sir Wilfrid Laurier started here, his coffin drawn in a carriage by a jet-black horse. By 1970 the further settling and shifting of foundations could no longer

*Appin Place, built 1868 and demolished in 1902.* NCC

be ignored: $6 million had to be spent on repairs, including a staggering $2.8 million to shore up the cracked, unstable foundations.

The land was formerly the site of Appin Place, the 1868 residence of Kathleen Stewart, whose husband, William, was a prosperous early Bytown merchant and councillor. He died in Toronto in 1856, championing Confederation and promoting Ottawa as capital. In 1834 the couple purchased the land bounded by Gladstone, the Rideau River and Bronson to just south of the Queensway. Kathleen Stewart built her home here after her husband's death in 1856. By the 1870s civil servants coming to the new capital started to purchase and build on the desirable lots, and in 1889 the City of Ottawa annexed what had become known as Stewarton with its population of 400 residents. *The Journal* of May 18, 1888, still referred Stewarton as "the outposts" of the city. In 1902 the federal government purchased and tore down Kathleen Stewart's Gothic cottage to make room for the museum as a part of the OIC's plan for Metcalfe Street.

Now walk north on Metcalfe Street. Number **306 Metcalfe** is **Birkett's Castle**, a whimsical home of bright red brick. A red sandstone archway framing the front door is handsomely set off by a strongly contrasting rough cut limestone base. The baronial Gothic style is emphasized by its deeply crenellated roofline reminiscent of

*306 Metcalfe, Birkett's Castle, is a residential interpretation of the castle theme. Oct. 1991.* K. Fletcher

*288 Metcalfe, First Church of Christ Scientist. Oct. 1991. K. Fletcher*

an old Scottish castle. Thomas Birkett was a successful hardware merchant in Ottawa, then mayor in 1891 and MP for Ottawa in 1900. He built the home in 1896, one of many VIPs to take up residence on the prestigious street.

Today, Birkett's Castle is home to Heritage Canada. The interior of the house still has much of its Victorian detailing. Reminiscent of the *chinoiserie* popular in Victorian times is the vestibule's pressed-tin panelling figured with oriental designs of birds, dragons and dolphins. The foyer boasts richly carved wooden paneling. A generous staircase sweeps into the hallway, and a bronze figurine of a fairy, Eau, graces the newel post.

Number **288 Metcalfe, First Church of Christ Scientist**, is an example of the Palladian classical tradition. Andrea Palladio was an Italian Renaissance architect whose style enthralled British architects in the 1700s. This 1913 church, by architect J. P. Maclaren, represents a revival of this temple-like classical style. It features strong vertical lines emphasized by solid Corinthian columns supporting a dominating triangular pediment. Curved arches over doorways and windows soften the stepped roof visible behind the pediment.

Number **233 Gilmour**, the **Public Service Alliance Building** (1968–69) at the corner of Gilmour and Metcalfe, is an oval tower faced in dark brick. It too is built on leda clay, but the architectural team of Schoeler, Heaton, Harvor and Menendez designed a raft-like reinforced foundation that "floats" the building on this unstable

*252 Metcalfe, the Laurentian Club, originally the home to J. R. Booth. Its irregular massing and eclectic use of materials and styles identify it as a late Queen Anne design. Aug. 1967. C. C. J. Bond. NCC, M. Newton file H12-122, Box 50*

deposit of clay. The building has evenly spaced windows whose glass is thicker in the top storeys to withstand the winds created by the building's shape.

Number **252 Metcalfe**, the **Laurentian Club**, was designed by architect John W. H. Watts for millionaire Ottawa Valley lumber baron John Rodolphus Booth in 1909. Booth hired Swedish craftsmen to do the interior woodwork. Each room features a different species of wood which Booth personally selected. He died here in 1925, aged ninety-five. His son, Jackson, continued to live in this eclectic Victorian home until its sale to the Laurentian Club in 1947.

A few steps farther south is **236 Metcalfe**, the **Chelsea Club**. This is one of the homes built on Ottawa Freehold Association property.

Note the contrasting coloured hooded mouldings that frame the windows on this Italianate residence. Round-headed dormers are set into the shallow roof, and slightly overhanging eaves are supported by carved wooden brackets. Sir Alexander Campbell, a Father of Confederation, is listed as the first of many residents. He sold to brewer Sir John Carling, who sold to Louis H. Davies, chief justice of the Supreme Court of Canada. The Chelsea Club purchased the home from Davies' executors in 1926.

Continue north on Metcalfe. The streetscape becomes increasingly confused as you pass from the last of the grand residences of Metcalfe into a profusion of competing apartment buildings, commercial properties and parking lots.

Before turning right (east) on Lisgar, look north to **180 Metcalfe** to see Noffke's 1928 **Medical Arts Building**, a six-storey edifice featuring a stepped effect characteristic of many skyscrapers of this period, such as Toronto's 1928–29 Royal York Hotel. Noffke's Art Deco design includes decorative, geometrical brickwork and façade pilasters that feature a linear motif at the top.

Now walk east to **182–184 Lisgar**. Two flanking gambrel-roofed gables softly flared at their base, and two porches with heavy brick and stone supports give a symmetrical look to this building. Its façade is enlivened by the polychromatic effect of the blond brick and grey stone. Horizontal planes are accentuated by the windows, the cornice and by alternate courses of stone and brick.

Number **180 Lisgar**, the **Royal York Apartments**, is next. Built in 1935, this is an unobtrusive building whose metal balcony railings feature a geometric Art Deco design. This motif is continued by the canopied entry with fluted, slightly projecting pilasters flanking the doorway, and by a stepped linear moulding above it.

Continue to Elgin Street, and turn left (north) towards the War Memorial and the start of your tour. To your immediate left is the tall post-modern **Barrister House**, **180 Elgin**, by architect Alistair Ross. Located across the street from the Ottawa Courthouse, the building was opened in 1985 as office space for barristers. Go inside to contrast the post-modernist interpretation of Art Deco, a style you have just seen on the exteriors of 180 Lisgar and Noffke's Medical Arts Building. Pilasters with flared capitals that incorporate lights inside them compete for your attention with the loud geometric patterns in the floor of highly polished, reflective marble.

Next door is **Place Bell Canada**, a 1971 Olympia and York development. The tall light-coloured towers, striped with dark windows, bring a vertical dimension to the streetscape, and are especially effective at night.

Number **150 Elgin**, is Dr. Grant's Home. James Alexander Grant was a much respected medical doctor at the turn of the century, physician to governors general from 1867 to 1905. *The Ottawa Citizen* of December 6, 1875, described Grant's new house: "Its style is that free and easy admixture of French Modern and Italian, which is fast becoming the vernacular of this county. The walls are of brick, Ottawa red, faced with Toronto white and with plain sandstone dressing to openings. It has a stone basement, measures 48 x 61 feet externally, and will cost about $11,000. The contractors are, for stonework, Messrs. Whillans. ... The architect is Mr. B. Billings." B. Billings was Braddish Billings III, the grandson of the Massachusetts settler who worked for Philemon Wright in 1817. He prospered and built the New England colonial clapboard home preserved as the Billings Museum.

Grant's home is an important survivor of the houses of the 1870s that once twinned Elgin with Metcalfe Street. Today the home is a restaurant. Go inside to see its interior layout, tall ceilings and the still-gracious staircase terminated by a sturdy newel post. Marble fireplaces still exist in most rooms.

*150 Elgin, Dr. Grant's home, was still flanked by a now-demolished red brick residence on Aug. 16, 1967. To the right is the spire of the First Baptist Church.*
C. C. J. Bond. NCC, M. Newton file, H12-135

Number **140 Laurier Avenue West, First Baptist Church**, graces the busy corner of Laurier and Elgin. Designed by architect James Mather in a Gothic style, the church was built in 1877–78. Tall lancet windows enhance the vertical thrust of the spire. Corner buttresses further emphasize this height. The cornerstone to Mather's cut lime-stone church was laid by Prime Minister Alexander Mackenzie. The stained glass north window honours the industry that developed the Ottawa Valley. Two lumber men stand beside an image of Christ, above the inscription: "The Trees of the Wood sing out in the Presence of the Lord."

Cross Laurier to the **Lord Elgin Hotel** built in 1940–41 by Ross and Macdonald in the châteauesque style with the copper turreted and dormered roof so favoured by Prime Minister Mackenzie King. Inside you will find marble busts of Lord and Lady Elgin. A newly refur-bished interior of rose and turquoise walls, marble columns and a coffered, lighted ceiling destroy whatever grace once existed inside its revolving front doors.

Continue north on Elgin to the **Lorne Building** at the northwest corner of Slater. Named after the Marquis of Lorne, governor general 1878–83 and a great patron of the arts, this building "temporarily" housed the National Gallery for more than thirty years. A 1977 competition for a new design was won by architect John Parkin and Associates, but construction never commenced. A second competi-tion, in 1982 and won by architect Moshe Safdie, resulted in the gallery's new home on Sussex Drive (*see* Sussex walk).

Continue along Elgin to Albert. The first **Knox Church** was erected in 1872 on this corner but was demolished to broaden Elgin Street in the 1930s, when Confederation Square was built. (The "new" 1932 Knox Church by architects Sproatt & Rolph is sited across from the Teachers' College on the southeast corner of Elgin and Lisgar.) Build-ing construction was supervised by J. Albert Ewart, and the builder was A. I. Garvock. The original design won an award from the Royal Architectural Institute of Canada.

This corner once overlooked the old post office, City Hall and Russell Hotel prior to their destruction by fire and demolition. *The Ottawa Citizen* of February 14, 1872, remarked: "The plans and specifi-cations of Knox's Church, which is to be built on Union Square, may be seen at Mr. Hope's stationery store. It will be an exceedingly handsome structure, and make quite an ornament to the city. If many more edifices be built in that neighbourhood, the old City Hall will crawl down to the Canal Basin and drown itself." This quote reflects

*Central Chambers c1920. Note the angled doorway, now removed.* NCC, M. Newton file, H12-221, Box 47

the keen interest Ottawans had in the development of their city. Many architects' plans were advertised in the pages of old newspapers.

Between Queen and Sparks stands **46 Elgin**, the **Central Chambers**, a triangular building of special heritage worth. It was erected in 1889 as prestigious office space. The architect was John James Browne of Montreal, who chose the highly decorative Queen Anne style – unusual for commercial buildings which were more commonly Italianate. It cost approximately $100,000. The Central Chambers is one of the first Ottawa buildings made with steel girders, which here rest on masonry supporting walls. The vertical composition of its bay windows represented another exciting design feature in its day. Here,

Browne copied the idea from British architect Richard Norman Shaw, whose 1871–73 New Zealand Chamber in London, England, was avant-garde at the time. Today, such a design is hardly noticed, as we are used to large expanses of glass. However, newspaper advertisements of the day boasted that the Central Chamber's windows were of the finest British plate glass.

The building was originally heated by steam, and tenants could choose whether to light their offices by electricity or gas. The *Ottawa Journal* of March 22, 1889, listed the Central Chambers advantages: "An Elevator of the newest and most approved design is in constant use. Special attention paid to ventilation and sanitary arrangements. Moderate rents will include janitorial service, thus relieving tenants of a very great annoyance."

Note the terracotta detailing of oak leaves, thistles and acorns along the building's polychromatic façade and the steeply gabled top windows that pierce the horizontal line of the flat-topped roof. This richly embellished building frames the west flank of Confederation Square beautifully. In 1964 the NCC purchased it. In January 1993, architects Brisbin, Brock and Benyan started work on refurbishing and integrating the Chambers into a large post-modern complex.

Just beyond the Central Chambers lies **48 Sparks**, the **Scottish Ontario Chambers**, at the south corner of the Sparks Street Mall. In 1883, architect William Hodgson designed it in the Italianate style – then the most popular architectural style for commercial properties. Victorians loved asymmetry and colour, here interpreted by the massive stone base supporting upper stories of lighter-looking polychromatic brickwork. Note the narrow windows which are highlighted by segmented voussoirs, with prominent central keystones.

Balancing it on the north corner of Sparks and Elgin is W. E. Noffke's 1938–39 **Central Post Office**, now **Postal Station B**, guarded by stone lions. Noffke's design effectively integrates with the other imposing stylistic precedents of the Langevin Block (Second Empire), East Block (Gothic Revival), Chateau Laurier (châteauesque) and Union Station (Classical).

The post office has three horizontal layers: a sturdy rusticated stone base sports two-storey high, rounded arch windows and is topped by a cornice above the second floor. Its mid-section features regularly spaced windows between flattened stone piers. This is surmounted by a copper châteauesque roof, its steep pitch relieved by dormer windows. Tying the vertical composition together is the

*Proud lion protecting the entrance to Noffke's Central Post Office, corner Sparks and Elgin.* NCC 172

curved corner. This is a successful *trompe-l'oeil*: it fools the onlooker into thinking it is a tower. Notice the angle of the corner curve as it extends upwards into the copper roofline. It has a triangular shape that resembles a corner tower.

Now you come to the **Langevin Block** built in 1883–89, designed by architect Thomas Fuller, who did the original Centre Block and Library of Parliament. This Second Empire building is of rich olive sandstone from New Brunswick. Its namesake, Sir Hector-Louis Langevin, was a Father of Confederation who represented New Brunswick. Like the post office, the Langevin Block is also a horizontally-layered composition rooted by a rusticated stone base. Prominent stringcourses divide the floors. Stand back to note how a vertical feeling is imparted by the fenestration: windows diminish in size from large ones on the lower floors to small ones on the top storey. Such details help to carry one's eye upwards and visually reduce what could otherwise be an overbearing horizontal massing. Notice the rounded arched windows that are framed by colonnettes of highly polished pink granite and prominent mouldings.

On your right is the War Memorial: you have now returned to the start of the canal walk.

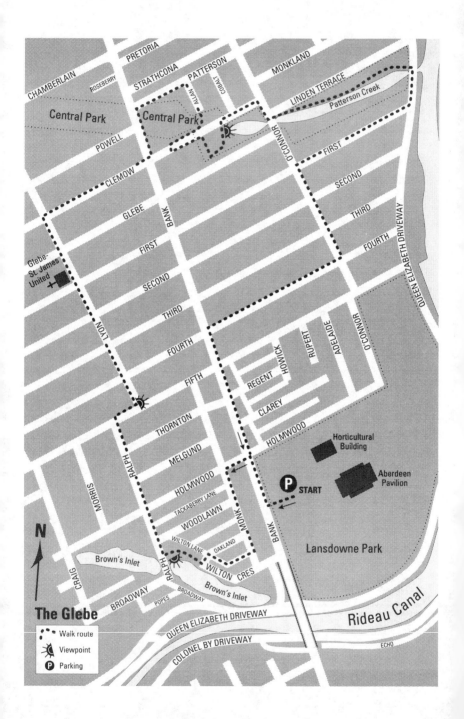

CHAMBERLAIN
ROSEBERRY
PRETORIA
STRATHCONA
PATTERSON
ALLAN
COBALT
MONKLAND
LINDEN TERRACE

Central Park
Central Park
Patterson Creek

POWELL
O'CONNOR
FIRST

CLEMOW
SECOND

GLEBE
BANK
THIRD
FOURTH

FIRST
QUEEN ELIZABETH DRIVEWAY

Glebe-
St. James
United
SECOND

THIRD
HOWICK
RUPERT
ADELAIDE
O'CONNOR

FOURTH

LYON
FIFTH
REGENT

THORNTON
CLAREY

RALPH
MELGUND
HOLMWOOD

MORRIS
HOLMWOOD
Horticultural
Building

TACKABERRY LANE
Aberdeen
Pavilion

WOODLAWN
MONK

P START

WILTON LANE
OAKLAND
BANK

Brown's Inlet
Lansdowne Park

N
RALPH
WILTON CRES

CRAIG
Brown's Inlet

BROADWAY
POPES
BROADWAY

QUEEN ELIZABETH DRIVEWAY
Rideau Canal

COLONEL BY DRIVEWAY
ECHO

**The Glebe**

- • • Walk route
- ☀ Viewpoint
- Ⓟ Parking

# The Glebe

## History

"New Toll Gate: The Ottawa and Gloucester Macadamized Road Company intend erecting a new toll gate house on their road opposite the residence of Mr. Mutchmore [sic]. This is done to catch those who evade the toll by branching off to Elgin near the Agricultural Show grounds."[12]

These two brief sentences from *The Ottawa Citizen* of 1875 open a window onto the land south of the McLeod Street "boundary" that on a 1874 Ottawa map is identified as the City Limit. Earlier, the McLeod toll gate officially delineated "country and city" until the 1880s. In later years, J. R. Booth's Canada Atlantic Railway similarly bisected the Glebe from Ottawa proper until it was replaced by the present Queensway in the 1950s.

In Ottawa's early years, the Glebe was farmland, much of it being part of the Clergy Reserve of St. Andrew's Presbyterian Church. In 1826, George Patterson, Colonel By's chief of the Commissariat, was also granted land in the area. But it was not until the 1870s that the farmland was deemed to be within reasonable distance from the city centre. Pioneer Alexander Mutchmor built his stone home, Abbotsford House, here in 1872 in open farmland.

*The Ottawa Citizen* of 15 May, 1874, listed a house for sale in the Glebe: "There are also excellent out-houses and every accommodation requisite for a comfortable rural residence ... an excellent opportunity for persons of limited means who desire to secure a pleasant Residence within a convenient distance of the city."

The exhibition grounds at Lansdowne Park became the ideal site for an agricultural fair, removed as it was from the city centre. From Buffalo Bill to the steeplechases and the first running of the Queen's Plate, the Glebe has long been dominated by its local fairs. Buffalo Bill Cody's "Wild West Show" first came to Ottawa in 1893 to thrill an astounded audience with its version of Custer's Last Stand at the Battle of the Little Bighorn. The troupe staged the show on the east side of the canal at the old Metropolitan Grounds past today's

Pretoria Bridge. In 1900 the famous scout returned to stage a second show to sellout crowds in the Glebe.

Mutchmor Driving Park was located west of Bank Street between First and Fifth, extending to Bronson. (Bank was first known as Esther Street, named for Colonel John By's wife.) Here, spectators bet on their favourite horse while watching the steeplechases. It was also home of the first running of Canada's premier horse race, the Queen's Plate, in 1872 and again in 1880. By the 1870s, residences started to pepper the mixed landscape of farmland, large gardened properties and fairgrounds south of the city limits.

As the city grew in the 1870s and 1880s, its southern expansion was inevitable. The attraction of the agricultural fairgrounds encouraged the development of the Bank Street road and Elgin Street, which were extended and bridges built over Patterson Creek.

The Mutchmor estate, an eight-room, one-and-a-half storey house, was built near the race track. In 1889 it came up for sale and was purchased as the Protestant Home for the Aged. A press release suggested: "it may reasonably be anticipated that before long the place will be conveniently accessible by means of street cars." By 1891 this was true. Thomas Ahearn drove the first tram from the Albert Street sheds of the Ottawa Electric Street Railway Company to Lansdowne Park. Thousands of spectators turned out to see this new contraption, the streetcar.

Although the streetcar was an undeniable boon, the design of the tracks – raised well above street level, not flush as they are in today's city streets – presented hazards to carters, pedestrians and horses throughout the city. Contemporary newspapers are full of complaints over the danger they represented to life and limb.

But the advent of these streetcars – the first in North America to be heated – meant people could now live in the areas previously considered remote countryside, such as the Glebe. But it only became a fashionable new neighbourhood after 1906, when the governor general's secretary built his home here, 126–128 Fourth Avenue.

At turn of the century, there were many homes between the canal and Bank Street, and First Avenue Public School had been built at First and O'Connor streets. However, on the west side of Bank through to Concession Street (Bronson) market gardens, pine trees and brush were punctuated by only a few buildings such as the Fourth Avenue Baptist Church and the Mutchmor Street School.

The Driveway, built by the Ottawa Improvement Commission (OIC) in 1900–05, allowed people to drive, first by horse and carriage,

*View of Central Park showing First Avenue Public School, c1911.* NCC 172

then by motorcar, to the developing residential area approaching Dow's Lake. The numbered streets (First to Fourth – Fifth Avenue was then called Mutchmor) were laid out by 1890, and by 1914 most Glebe streets were built. The area developed steadily, especially after World War I, when returning soldiers urgently required housing.

As the city grew, the OIC gave more attention to the creation of public parks. Parks were increasingly considered critical open spaces. OIC planner Frederick Todd was responsible for saving the land either side of Patterson Creek from construction, and for turning it into a park in the early 1900s.

After World War I, the Glebe prospered, and properties adjacent to the OIC's landscaped drives became desirable residential locations. Clemow Avenue, Brown's Inlet and Patterson Creek were the locations of choice for estate houses designed by architects such as W. E. Noffke, who was hired to design a planned community of houses nestled around Central Park.

But the Glebe's residential development was dominated by members of the new, increasingly sophisticated middle class, who had specific needs but not the money to engage a personal designer such as Noffke. Nor did they have the income to hire servants. This need spawned a new breed of architect, a new design philosophy, and a new type of housing that incorporated such comforts as interior bathrooms, central heating and electricity.

In the late 1920s and the 1930s, Glebe developers such as David Younghusband purchased large blocks of property, building "Glebe charmers" such as 394 Third (not on this tour). Now that the Glebe had become a trendy part of town instead of sleepy rural countryside, the city started to impose restrictions upon what type of structure could be built. A deed of sale, dated April 14, 1927, dictated that foundations had to be of stone or concrete, and the home "constructed of brick, brick veneer, stone, stucco or concrete; each dwelling to cost not less than $5,000." This sum is considerably less than the $10,000 minimum mentioned in a Rockcliffe deed of sale, dated 1910.

After World War II, mass production, the development of prefabricated construction techniques and other technological innovations swept the building and architectural professions. The new fashion became the bungalow: so it was that the Glebe lost its attraction as a residential area during the 1950s. People looked for newer homes, larger lots, more modern schools and shopping plazas. The Billings Bridge and Alta Vista suburbs were developed in the 1950s. Many Glebe homes were converted into apartments.

At the same time, the Glebe's population changed from being largely British Protestant to a mixture of ethnic groups. Fashion swings being what they are, the Glebe enjoyed a rediscovery in the 1960s and 1970s, as owner-residents returned to "gentrify" the neighbourhood. Older homes were purchased, renovated, and often restored to single family dwellings. But the Glebe's new popularity has brought the headaches of traffic control, high-rise development and heritage conservation.

### Neighbourhood Styles

The Glebe is a community of middle-class homes characterized by closed-in front porches, red brick walls and gambrel and gable roofs. Most are two-and-a-half or three stories high. Interspersed among these typical houses are examples of Prairie and Spanish Revival designs, with their horizontal planes and red roof tiles. Tall apartment towers dot the streetscape, but are kept to a minimum by strict zoning bylaws. The Glebe, like many other Ottawa neighbourhoods, possesses an active community association that keeps current councillors in tune with the varied residential, schooling and commercial interests of the neighbourhood.

Density and traffic control are key issues as witnessed by the special studies by architects and planners such as Glebe resident John

*Natural cedar summerhouse handmade by OIC carpenter Thomas Craig, c1911.*
NCC 061-38

Leaning. Heritage is another reoccurring concern, which climaxed in the 1968 fight to save Pretoria Bridge. This cause coalesced the efforts of several community groups throughout the city, which united in an effort to prevent a traffic corridor from further separating the Glebe from Ottawa South.

In the early 1970s, Glebe residents banded together to protest the rapidly advancing high-rise apartment buildings marching down the west side of the Canal. In August 1974, the Ontario Municipal Board approved a down-zoning of several blocks between Patterson Creek and Fifth Avenue. The decision did not prevent William Teron's hotly contested tower at 300 the Driveway (1974), but it did stop the demolition of the picturesque Rogue Victorian row house complex to its south.

Of similar heritage concern has been the fate of Moses C. Edey's Aberdeen Pavilion and Francis Sullivan's Horticultural Building. These buildings have been the focus of an ongoing preservation battle. To date, the grand reopening of a stabilized Aberdeen Pavilion is expected in spring of 1994.

*Detail of the Aberdeen Pavilion, south entry. Note the laughing horse's head (top) and the lion's head (bottom). Oct. 1991.* K. Fletcher

## Walk Tips

4.5 km; 2 hours.
The Glebe walk takes you past urban parks, waterways and shaded streets. Bank Street is the main north-south artery bisecting the neighbourhood. It is a commercial street, made up of shops, libraries, churches, neighbourhood cafés and pubs. Washrooms exist in the many restaurants and businesses along Bank. Fifth Avenue Court at Fifth and Bank Streets, has a public washroom and a pleasant interior courtyard, a welcome refuge in inclement weather.

## The Walk

Park at Lansdowne Park, the original exhibition grounds and the heart of the Glebe, and walk east to the 1898 **Aberdeen Pavilion**, the **Cattle Castle**. It is easily recognizable by its rounded roof topped by a cupola ringed with snarling lions heads. Designed by Shawville, Quebec, architect Moses C. Edey, the Aberdeen Pavilion is a rare surviving example of exhibition halls inspired by the Crystal Palace, built for the 1851 London Great Exhibition. Edey's design took only two months to erect, an event that amazed Ottawans.

The building is an important engineering achievement in Ottawa. It represents the first use in the city of long-span steel arches, which create an open interior eminently suitable for agricultural displays. Steel's structural strength allowed Edey to design an interior enclosure 310 feet long with a span of more than 130 feet. His use of steel with pressed-tin cladding tells us he was building with permanence

*The* Maude *and two other side-wheel steamers unloaded fair-goers where Fifth Ave. now joins the Driveway. From* Canadian Illustrated News *October 16, 1879.* NCC 172

in mind. In 1899, during the Boer War, Lord Strathcona's Horse Regiment camped inside the building for two weeks before being sent to the front. And it was here the Silver Seven won the 1903 Stanley Cup.

On the outside, the two cross-gabled side entries to the north and south are particularly decorated, highlighted by corner towers that are topped by cupolas. Its southern entrance has the projecting head of a laughing horse over the central doorway; the balancing north door sports a cow's head. The east and west doorways are less fanciful but their pediments and round-arched windows still evoke a sense of whimsy.

Of a completely different style is Francis C. Sullivan's **Horticultural Building**, just north of the Aberdeen Pavilion. Sullivan worked for Moses Edey for several years, but their designs could not be more different. Unfortunately, the only commonality their buildings share is a seemingly incessant threat of demolition.

Stand back to appreciate this building's stark horizontal lines, a true example of Sullivan's interpretation of the Prairie design of Frank Lloyd Wright. Horizontal planes are accentuated by the flat roof and its broad eaves, as well as by flanking wings that carry the eye outwards. Exposed concrete spandrels serve to emphasize the linear motif. Note, too, Sullivan's detail in the façade and window treatment. Built in 1914, the building is an important example of a commercial structure after the Prairie School style.

Walk back to Bank, head right (north) and cross the street at the stoplights at Holmwood. Stop at the old stone house at **954 Bank**, **Abbotsford House**, now part of the **Glebe Centre**. This lovely stone residence, built in 1872 for Alexander Mutchmor, was named after Sir Walter Scott's birthplace. In 1889, the house became the Protestant Home for the Aged. *The Ottawa Journal* of August 23, 1889, reported that the home, on its two-and-a-quarter-acre property, "is capable of accommodating about 75 inmates, and is surrounded by a beautiful growth of shade trees. ... About $10,000 will be required to pay for the property and place it in a proper condition for occupation." On September 3 that year the paper reported that Moses C. Edey had been asked to prepare an estimate of the cost of repairs.

Its Victorian Gothic design features steeply pitched gables set off by delicately turned bargeboard. The projecting bay window fronting Bank Street and the multiple gables add a note of charm to the streetscape. Under threat of demolition for years, Abbotsford House is now recognized as a heritage property.

Turn left (west) on Holmwood to the first street, Monk, and again turn left (south). Keep your eyes peeled for **Wilton Lane** (*not* Wilton Crescent), which leads off to the right, one building past Oakland. Walk up the lane to appreciate the Glebe's back-garden atmosphere. Gardens are defined by fences, but most are at a convenient height that fosters the neighbourly conversation that binds a community together.

Stop at the corner of Oakland for a moment to note the clapboard garages and also the horse and sulky weathervane atop **25 Oakland's** garage.

Turn left on Oakland and almost immediately right onto a walkway bordering **Brown's Inlet**. Houses crowd the edge of the inlet, each with a splendid southern view. In midsummer yellow water lilies carpet the inlet, in fall the water reflects the season's glorious colours, and in winter young hockey players shout and dash about on the ice. Walk to Ralph Street, directly ahead. Pause to look southeast to the Bank Street Bridge designed by Newton J. Ker in 1912. You can also spy the silver dome of the 1914 Monastery of the Precious Blood, built upon "Ray's Hill," once a popular tobogganing run. J. Albert Ewart's 1931 Southminster United Church is also visible, as is his companion piece across Bank, the Ottawa Library South Branch.

*86–88 Ralph, Oct. 1991. The Baker residence is now a double, overlooking Brown's Inlet.* K. Fletcher

Turn right on Ralph, walking north to see your first W. E. Noffke Glebe design, **86–88 Ralph**, the **Baker residence**. The urns carefully placed at intervals along the front entryway, the Spanish tiled roof, and the sheer stucco walls are vintage Noffke. The view of Brown's Inlet from this elegant house is today obscured by the townhouse complex at **92–94 Ralph**. This is a good example of how lot severance permanently changes the face of a neighbourhood. Typical of his best designs, Noffke's original design of 86–88 Ralph created a house organically sited and proportioned to its lot. Today's infill buildings destroy the grace of the house.

Continue to **20 Ralph**, **Berwick Cottage**, built in 1895. The cottage's original façade is now much altered.

At Fifth Avenue, cross the street and head to your right (east). **Mutchmor School**, **185 Fifth**, takes its name from the first owner of Abbotsford House and was built in the same year as Berwick Cottage. Originally a four-room schoolhouse, it was designed by architect E. L. Horwood and cost $10,470.

The school is an example of Romanesque Revival design. It features squared-off towers, horizontal massing accentuated by the low-pitched roof, symmetrical alignment of windows, and contrasting broad horizontal stone stringcourses beneath the second-floor windows. The central doorway's massive rounded archway is the school's most identifiable Romanesque feature. The rounded second-storey windows above the entry echo this dramatic arch. Note, too, the Romanesque terracotta capitals on either side of the doorway piers. Terracotta became increasingly popular in the 1870s in North America, and was locally available to Ottawa builders from Thomas Clark's brick and terracotta yards in New Edinburgh.

From here, look east down Fifth Avenue towards Bank. Note the tongue-and-groove enclosed verandahs that front some of the red brick, three-storey gambrel and gable roofed homes: this is a typical Glebe streetscape. The verandahs provide welcome additional living space. Storm windows can be removed during summer to create screened porches.

Turn left (north) on Lyon Street. Between Fourth and Third, on your left (west) is Corpus Christi School, built in 1926.

Note the solid massing of **690 Lyon**, the **Glebe Community Centre** (built in 1924 as St. James Methodist Church). A Classical design typical of the early twentieth-century revivalist movement, this Roman temple-like structure features monumental Doric columns topped by a triangular pediment around its original main entrance on Second Ave. The domed roof created for the original church is a Glebe landmark.

The revivalists sought change. They espoused a return to cleanly defined lines, in stark contrast to the fanciful, ornate detailing of Queen Anne and Victorian Gothic styles. Yet, in the years just before and after World War I, most architects continued their backward glance for inspiration. There were not many who strode forwards as progenitors of the soon-to-emerge modernist movement. The Glebe Community Centre is a stylistic contemporary of the 1909–12 Union Station (*see* Sussex walk); the 1904 Tabaret Hall (*see* Sandy Hill walk) and the 1913 First Church of Christ Scientist (*see* Canal walk). Each is an important reminder of its architect's struggle for purity of structural expression. If it is open, go inside the Community Centre to see the interior of the dome.

Back outside, continue along Lyon, past its typical Glebe row houses to **662 Lyon**, first built in 1914 as the **Ottawa Ladies' College** (originally located at the Ottawa Technical School on Bay and Albert Streets in Upper Town). During the Depression years the residential school suffered declining enrollment, and in 1942 the building was expropriated. During World War II it served as the Glebe Barracks for the Canadian Women's Army Corps. Later it also served as the original site of Carleton University. Today it provides administrative offices for the Ottawa Board of Education.

The building itself has a vague Spanish Revival feel. Of note are the overhanging eaves with their bold wooden bracket supports. Snow guards, which look like a low wrought-iron fence, march around the roofline.

Directly opposite, at **650 Lyon**, is **Glebe-St. James United Church**. Designed by architect J. W. H. Watts, it opened its doors in May 1906. Its fanciful turrets of shingled siding are painted moss green and beautifully complement the soft grey trim and limestone walls. Note in particular the transept tower: this is a Romanesque feature both in its positioning and massing.

It was originally Glebe-St. James Presbyterian church prior to the amalgamation of the Methodists, Congregationalists and Presbyterians into the United Church in 1925. After Union, this corner of the Glebe had two United churches separated by only one city block. In December 1970, the two congregations decided to join forces. One of the churches became the Community Centre at 690 Lyon, which you have just passed. The other, now Glebe-St. James, continues as a United church and also houses Ottawa's Korean Community Church.

*Glebe-St. James United Church, Oct. 1991.* K. Fletcher

Walk two blocks farther north to Clemow Avenue, named after Francis Clemow, who was managing director of the Consumers' Gas Company in the mid-1800s, and a senator from 1885 to 1902. It was Clemow who urged that Ottawa's first waterworks be constructed.

Turn right (east) on Clemow. Here the large residences are fronted by deep gardens, removing them from the curious eyes of sidewalk amblers. Tastefully designed traffic barriers barely concealed as plant boxes restrict car access from Bank Street. Clemow is another enclave of embassy residences. As you walk towards Bank Street various styles compete for attention, from the Palladian classicism of **211 Clemow**, to the bell-capped copper turret of **164 Clemow**. The globe street lamps along Clemow, rather than any stylistic conformity in its houses, provide visual continuity to the streetscape.

Clemow was one of Frederick Todd's planned boulevards of dist-inction for the capital. He was a stickler for detail and included such details as the height of fences, planting of trees and size restrictions for billboards in his plans.

Turn left on Bank and cross the bridge spanning the filled-in westerly extension of Patterson Creek – Central Park.

On the west side of Bank, north of the Park, is **672 Bank, Ambassador Court**, designed by W. E. Noffke for developer David Epstein in 1928. The wedge-shaped plan is flush to both Central Park and Bank Street, and the end-corner is squared-off with small projecting balconies. There is a strong cornice with a pedimented parapet that breaks the flat roofline. Concrete stringcourses between stories contrast with the yellow brick walls, and the arched front entryway adds visual interest. When it was first opened, an advertised feature of the Ambassador Court was that every apartment had its own electric fireplace.

Cross Bank Street at the lights and walk east on Patterson, one of the oldest streets in the Glebe. There are several flat-topped row houses near Bank Street on the north side of Patterson, and on the south is a new, two-layered infill complex called **Central Park**, at **204–226 Patterson**. Farther along, row housing gives way to vernacular red brick houses with steeply gabled roofs so typical of this neighbourhood. Some of these homes feature the irregular massing characteristic of the Queen Anne style, especially where Patterson continues east towards the canal, a section this tour does not include.

Turn right on Allan Place. Number **6 Allan Place** is attributed to architect Francis C. Sullivan. The original design has been much altered by a front addition.

Number **12 Allan Place** is W. E. Noffke's 1913 Prairie School house designed for Ernest C. Powell, (brother of W. F. Powell, the developer of Patterson Creek). This house takes full advantage of its raised elevation overlooking the east portion of Central Park. The home has an unmistakable Japanese feel, which is derived from wide, low-pitched eaves with carved, flared rafter ends. They are painted a rich reddish-brown, a colour common to Japanese lacquer work. In both form and colour such details evoke a Japanese shrine. This is no fanciful coincidence: Frank Lloyd Wright spent several years in Japan and was heavily influenced by that country's architectural styles. Thus, Japanese motifs crept into Wright's plans. Because Noffke (and Sullivan) were influenced by this great American architect, their own architectural designs, in turn, re-interpreted Japanese form so that today, we can observe them here in the Glebe.

Descend the few steps into the park. It is here, in the carefully landscaped parkland of **Patterson Creek** and **Central Park** that Noffke made his major impression upon the Glebe. Developer W. F. Powell and his aunt, Adelaide Clemow, hired the prolific Ottawa architect to design an integrated, prestigious development here. Noffke's 1913 plans, still extant, reveal his sensitivity to site.

On your immediate left at the foot of the stairs is a grey stone "castle" residence of block construction. Notice it sports the typical battlement feature, a corbelled parapet, and that it has two corner

*27 Clemow, the second home Noffke designed for developer W. F. Powell. Oct. 1991. K. Fletcher*

towers, one round, the other octagonal. Its lovely front door has a beautiful oval, bevelled glass inset.

Keep to your right on the park footpath. Then climb the steps beside **27 Clemow**, the Tudor Revival second house Noffke designed for **William F. Powell**. The house integrates well to the hillside. Half-timbering indicates the Tudor inspiration, a style emphasized by the leaded glass windows with their wrought iron detailing. Twin chimneys with copper flashing lend the house its old English cottage appeal.

Opposite is **26 Clemow**, the dramatically different Noffke house built in the Spanish Colonial Revival style in 1926 for **Levi W. Crannell**. The house features a sheer white stucco finish, spiral colonnettes and red tiled roof. Note its round-headed windows and the dramatic off-centred chimney with flared base that is the dominant feature of the front façade. A curved parapet gable over the main door completes the ornate façade.

Turn left to view **20 Clemow**, Noffke's own home, which he built in 1913. Noffke left his "cottage" home at 209 Wilbrod in Sandy Hill to reside here for several years. Perhaps he designed this to advertise his considerable design talents: it is certainly a potpourri of styles. Basically, it represents the increasingly popular bungalow style with a broad front porch and wide, gable dormer above it. Yet there are Tudor touches in the arched, buttressed and battlemented front entrance. And Noffke reminds everyone of his competency in Spanish Colonial Revival style by adding familiar red roof tiles and a massive chimney. Note, too, the geometric designs in the brickwork.

Another Tudor Revival is **18 Clemow**, Noffke's 1923 design for Ethel Chamberlain's home, which nicely balances **27 Clemow** across the street.

Now turn left (east) towards Patterson Creek and walk up the gentle grassy slope on your right. From here you can see what is perhaps Noffke's most successful design, **85 Glebe Avenue, W. F. Powell's** first home on the park built in 1913. An Ottawa landmark, this house is best seen from Glebe Avenue, a few paces ahead.

The house's flaring buttresses and horizontal planes deliberately carry the eye from the line of the house into the surrounding trees and parkland. The home is truly *part of* its setting. Note the *porte-cochère*, or covered entrance, that shelters the front door on the semi-circular drive. In contrast, the row of steeply pitched, gable-roofed homes on the southern side of Glebe Avenue dominate the streetscape rather than fitting into it.

Now retrace your steps, returning to Patterson Creek and the south side of Clemow. Spend a moment to look east past O'Connor Street to the canal to savour the precious open space preserved in the heart of the city.

*85 Glebe, Jan. 1992. Note its flaring* porte-cochère. E. Fletcher

Continue east to **11 Clemow**, the **Benson C. Beach House**, at the corner of Cobalt. Noffke designed this house in 1915 for the president of the Beach Foundry. Its yellow brick lightens the mass of this residence. The projecting porch piers and the chimney introduce strong vertical lines into a structure which otherwise appears solid and massive. Proceed to O'Connor Street, where you will view the last three Noffke designs of Patterson Creek.

Number **1 Clemow**, the **High Commission of Ghana**, is Noffke's 1915 design for Francis X. Plaunt, a railway tie contractor. Noffke historian Shannon Ricketts describes 1 Clemow as being Mediterranean style after a turn-of-the-century, exclusive Florida resort named Coral Gables. This house features sheer white stucco, unembellished windows and the remnants of its original red tile roof.

Across the street is **515 O'Connor** at the corner of Monkland, the 1913 Noffke design for **Austin E. Blount**, Prime Minister Sir Robert Borden's private secretary. The house is now the Tunisian Embassy.

Nicely complementing Blount's home is **517 O'Connor**, the G. Frederick Hodgins' home, also 1913 by Noffke. Whereas 515 is a solid looking stone structure, quite different in feeling from the other Noffke designs on Patterson Creek, Number 517 possesses a few features that suggest Frank Lloyd Wright's Prairie Style. Horizontal planes are highlighted by a masonry base topped by a narrow stucco

*Monkland Avenue, summer 1911. Prior to the Noffke-Powell development, these landscaped drives had few homes.* NCC 062-8

*517 O'Connor. Oct. 1991.* K. Fletcher

strip on the upper level. The effect is finished with a low pitched roof. One-storey wing extensions on either side of the house carry the eye even more linearly: on the left is a covered doorway (another *porte-cochère*), on the right, an enclosed porch. Also reminiscent of Prairie Style are the projecting vertical piers topped with a spherical orna-ment. However, what is definitely "un-Wrightian" are the parapeted end-gables with chimneys.

Now turn right on O'Connor. Just south of Linden Terrace find the path beside Patterson Creek. Walk due east toward the Driveway. Note the large homes lining Linden Terrace, some of which have massive column supports to their front porches. On the south side of the inlet, you can see the backs of homes on First Avenue. As you get closer to the Driveway, you can see the tile-roofed National Capital Commission service building just below the bridge. Built in the days of the Federal District Commission (heir to the Ottawa Improvement Commission) around 1928, its design is attributed to Francis Sullivan. Similar structures are found in Rockcliffe Park.

Climb the stairs. Turn right (south) on the Driveway, crossing the little bridge over Patterson Creek, also credited to Sullivan. In 1904, American historian, raconteur and traveller Anson A. Gard revealed a hidden feature of the uppermost iron tube rail along the canal. An invention of local iron worker J. L. Flanders, the rail doubled as a water pipe, complete with attachments for hoses. It was an ingeniously designed sprinkler system.

Number **300 the Driveway** is a tall apartment building built in 1974 by William Teron's firm, Urbanetics. It is a typical Teron highrise with dark brown brick and horizontal, angled pre-cast concrete balconies. This highrise was bitterly opposed by many Glebe residents who sought to prevent the march of highrises southwards along the canal. Beside its western face, along First, are low townhouses, overlooking Patterson Creek.

Directly across from number 300, on the south corner at First Avenue, is **304–312 the Driveway**. This whimsical row house development was spared demolition by the Ontario Municipal Board's down-zoning ruling of August, 1974. The 1906 design continues the Victorian love for asymmetrical juxtapositioning of forms. Here, porthole windows compete with arch-roofed and bell-capped turrets, and a staggered, zig-zag ground floor plan not only gives a modicum of privacy to each entry, but also exploits to excellent advantage the awkwardly narrow, angled lot.

Turn right (west) on First Avenue. As you pass by 304–312 on your left you can see more clearly the zig-zag pattern of its plan.

Farther along are **49A** and **49B First**. These 1990 infill houses are a "second layer" of buildings behind the older homes fronting the street. Number 300 the Driveway, its neighbouring townhouses, and this double layer of homes along First are all evidence of the resurgence in popularity of the Glebe as a residential neighbourhood.

Numbers **70** and **74 First** are two charming clapboard homes. Their simple façades and attractive verandah detailing provide visual relief from the red brick that distinguishes Glebe streets.

Number **73 First**, **First Avenue Public School**, was built in 1898 as an eight-room schoolhouse. At that time, Patterson Creek was wooded. Designed by J. Albert Ewart, son of architect David Ewart, the school cost $20,484. The completion of this school and the 1895 Mutchmor School within four years of one another attests to the growing population of the Glebe area at the turn of the century.

The school features a massive Romanesque arched entryway and terracotta faces of the West Wind on either side of the portal. The building has weathered many alterations, including the addition of a ventilation system in 1907 and, in 1936, the twin conveniences of new wiring and urinals in the washrooms. In recent years a gymnasium has been added at the rear, designed by Alistair Ross and Associates and built of red clay brick.

*49A and 49B First Ave. are second-layer infill facing Patterson Creek, behind 49 First. Oct. 1991. K. Fletcher*

Turn left (south) on O'Connor. Pass the imposing **Prince Rupert Apartments, 585 O'Connor,** built around 1915. It features symmetrical four-storey bay windows and deeply recessed balconies with prominent wooden railings. Ornate brackets support the cornices of this flat-topped, four-storey walk-up.

Now turn right (west) down Fourth Avenue. Here you find an assortment of end-gabled red brick homes, many enlivened by wooden porches fancifully decorated with motifs such as sunbursts, moons and stars.

Number **91A Fourth** is the **Religious Society of Friends** (Quakers) meeting house. The second church in the Glebe, the original 1892

*Terracotta detailing of the West Wind on First Avenue Public School. Oct. 1991.*
K. Fletcher

structure was wooden. In about 1910, it became the Zion Congrega-
tional Church, and around that time was clad in brick. In 1969, the
Society of Friends purchased it and used it as their meeting hall. In
the late 1980s the Friends sold off the western section which was
subsequently redesigned by architect Wolfgang Mohaupt, who developed the site with infill housing. The congregation now meets in the
eastern, rear brick extension.

At the northwest corner of Bank and Fourth look across to the
**Fourth Avenue Baptist Church**. Two lots were purchased here
around 1898 for $2,200 and soon a small wooden church opened its
doors. It was a lonely building, just about the only one built at that
time between Bank and Bronson. This red brick church was erected
in 1904.

Now turn left (south) on Bank towards Lansdowne Park and the
start of this walk. You pass **Fifth Avenue Court** on your left, at the
corner of Bank and Fifth. This complex integrates old shopfronts with
a new rear, interior covered courtyard. It won an Award of Excellence
for Minto developers in 1980. Yet it is an interesting example of how
even the small-scaled suburban covered mall concept can fail when
transplanted into an established community neighbourhood. In the
friendly, "laid-back" Glebe, people like to shop on the street, happily

wandering in and out of their favourite stores where shopowners are friends. This covered courtyard with its interior stores is simply alien to the neighbourhood ambiance.

Continue south on Bank to return to your car and the start of this walk at Lansdowne Park.

*585 O'Connor, the Prince Rupert Apartments. Oct. 1991.* K. Fletcher

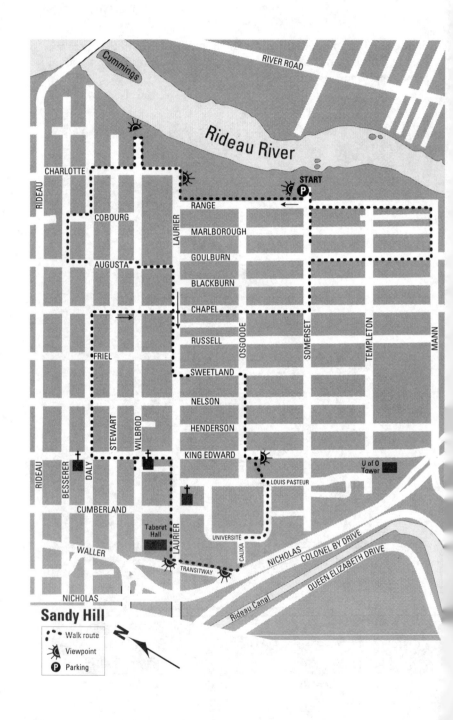

RIVER ROAD

Cummings

Rideau River

CHARLOTTE

RIDEAU

COBOURG

LAURIER

START
P

RANGE

MARLBOROUGH

GOULBURN

AUGUSTA

BLACKBURN

CHAPEL

FRIEL

RUSSELL

OSGOODE

SOMERSET

TEMPLETON

MANN

SWEETLAND

NELSON

STEWART

WILBROD

HENDERSON

KING EDWARD

LOUIS PASTEUR

U of O
Tower

RIDEAU

BESSERER

DALY

CUMBERLAND

Taberet
Hall

LAURIER

UNIVERSITÉ

CALIXA

NICHOLAS

COLONEL BY DRIVE

WALLER

TRANSITWAY

QUEEN ELIZABETH DRIVE

NICHOLAS

Rideau Canal

**Sandy Hill**

- Walk route
- Viewpoint
- P Parking

N

# Sandy Hill

## History

Sandy Hill's building boom started in the 1860s after Ottawa was declared the capital of Canada. Middle and upper class Canadians moved to the city to take up civil service jobs, and, very soon, the city ran out of suitable housing for them. In 1876 the land south of Laurier Street East, lying between King Edward and Chapel – part of Colonel By's estate – was surveyed. From the outset, lots were kept large to accommodate "villa residences" and sold by private sale only to create an exclusive domain for the wealthy.

Yet there were problems. Among the most humbling was the stench of the drains, which disgusted Sir John A. Macdonald at Stadacona Hall as much as it did the ordinary mortal. His next-door neighbour, architect Colborne (Coly) P. Meredith, provided a sobering glimpse into the Sandy Hill of the 1870s in his unpublished memoirs. Commonly, drains were of the primitive wooden box variety. Even if they were made from tile, most joints were of clay, not cement. As a result, they often failed, sometimes forcing families to vacate their homes. Meredith observed that children continually suffered from sore throats, and that the relationship of health to inadequate sanitation was not properly understood.

Rats were another pernicious problem. Backyard stables provided a handy food source for these vermin, and basements were often floored with cedar sleepers, allowing space beneath them for the rats to create runways and nests. (Interestingly, the 1990s environmental phenomenon of the backyard compost pile has lured rats back into many Ottawa residential communities.)

Streets and sidewalks posed their own hazards. Plank sidewalks heaved and created a jumble of levels. Just as today, residents were responsible for shovelling the snow in front of their own home. Even back "in the good old days," human nature being what it is, some people were more diligent than others, resulting in a haphazard pattern of cleared space and deep snow. Frequently, pedestrians on snowshoes competed on the roads with horse-drawn sleighs and wagons. However, winter's packed snow provided a far preferable road surface than the muddy potholes of spring and blowing dust of summer.

Sandy Hill may not have been ideal, but lots were of good size, and during the 1860s and 1870s many houses were built. Coly Meredith recalled his family's 1874 home at the northwest corner of Augusta and Wilbrod as being on the fringe of Ottawa. It bordered unfenced meadows extending to the Rideau River, which provided grazing for residents' cattle.

Ottawa's last smallpox epidemic was in 1874. Irish labourers were decimated by the disease, which spread with lightning speed through their log shanty homes bordering the Canal and in Lowertown. The epidemic touched all parts of the city, and Sandy Hill was no exception. In 1875 *The Ottawa Citizen* carried a story about the Sandy Hill hospital operated by the Grey Nuns, which "has been converted into a small pox ward. The old wooden building should be destroyed as soon as possible."

The need for a hospital was great, and the nuns were determined to erect a new hospital in the community. But many residents were opposed, and newspapers of the day reflected their strong feelings. The July 8, 1875, *Citizen* tried to quell concerns about contamination,

*Strathcona Park, c1905. Note the park's ornate pathways and artificial streams with ornamental bridges.* NCC 061-28

but was unsuccessful. Construction commenced on the new hospital, but on July 15 a passionate objector who understood little about explosives, tried to blow it up, unsuccessfully.

There were other protests when the old wooden hospital in Sandy Hill was torn down. The wood was supposed to be burned but instead was sold to someone who intended to build. Again the Sandy Hill community united and successfully forced the hapless buyer to burn the "infected timbers." Residents repeatedly took matters into their own hands regarding the Nun's hospital. As late as November 22, 1879, the story resurfaces: the 1875 hospital was burned to the ground by "residents of the locality."

Today, Sandy Hill residents continue their participation in the protection of the community – but modern methods exclude explosives. Instead, protection through bylaws seems to do the trick, in combination with an active community organization. The 1982 City Bylaws list four bylaws that mark the creation of several Sandy Hill heritage districts. The designated areas vary in size from a single lot to many blocks.

Another contentious issue was a 1991 proposal to build a shelter for homeless women at 229 Chapel Street. In spring of 1993 this house, the Frederick Toller house, still remains vacant. Sandy Hill residents opposed to the shelter's location were able to convince the Ontario Municipal Board that their neighbourhood has its share of housing for the needy. *The Ottawa Citizen* of February 20, 1993, reported that owner Eric Cohen now may be obliged to convert the residence to a "rooming house for as many as 42 tenants." Whether it is turned into a shelter or rooming house, transformation of Toller house will adversely affect neighbourhood density.

## Neighbourhood Styles

Vernacular Victorian Gothic cottages, personal residences that several Ottawa architects (Noffke, Ewart, Sullivan, Meredith) designed for themselves, and the micro-community of University of Ottawa are among the landmarks greeting the Sandy Hill walker. As well, Sandy Hill presents two uncommon modernist residences for explorers to enjoy towards the end of this delightful ramble.

It is a diverse neighbourhood of museums, embassies, private homes and apartments. At its southern extremity, Mann Road, are a series of CMHC public housing units that border the noisy Queensway. On the restful banks of the Rideau River, Strathcona Park provides shaded pathways and pretty views. Bordering this park are the

Embassy residences that were once single-family homes. And, on top of the rise of land overlooking the Park is the much altered, once stately Munross House, former home of lumber baron John Mather and now a private club, Le Cercle. East of this building are a series of heritage structures including Laurier House, former home to prime ministers Sir Wilfrid Laurier and Mackenzie King.

As its name suggests, Sandy Hill sits on underground deposits of sand, which challenged the architects and builders of this neighbourhood much as the leda clay made building difficult in old Stewarton (*see* Canal walk).

## Walk Tips

7 km; 4 hours.
Strathcona Park's beautiful landscaped lawns make it a delightful start and end to this walk. In summer, the low water level of the Rideau River entices many to cross to far side where the bubble tennis courts of the Rideau Tennis Club are located. Sandy Hill has many corner stores and public buildings, so you will find a spot to rest and linger over a coffee. And be sure to go inside Laurier House Museum for a peek into the private lives of prime ministers Laurier and King.

## The Walk

Park your car in the lot at the easternmost extension of Somerset East, in Strathcona Park.

Walk north on Range, keeping the sparkling Rideau River to your right. (The lovely paths of Strathcona Park provide a shaded, lovely start to the walk, too. You could walk through the park rather than the street, and look over at the homes fronting Range.)

Strathcona Park has enjoyed various former lives. At first it was the neighbourhood commons and cow pasture. By 1891 it was a fifty-acre, nine-hole golf course developed by Hugh Renwick. Coly Meredith's memoirs reveal he changed the name Salisbury Road to Range Road to honour the park's third life as the Dominion Rifle Range which opened in 1873. As you walk north, look at the homes framing the park.

Number **32 Range**, the **Venezuelan Ambassador's residence**, was built in 1930 by the firm of Noffke, Morin and Sylvester as home for a Gerald Bate, Esq. It is a two-storey, gable-roofed stone cottage, complete with stone walls delineating the property line. Its two chimneys highlight the end gables, and its central entryway is framed by sidelight windows and an Adamesque elliptically shaped fanlight over the door. To accent the symmetrical design of the house, an oval "porthole" window is centred above the fanlight.

Number **28 Range** is the 1924 **J. R. Booth Jr. residence**, a Spanish Colonial Revival design by architects Burritt and Kingston. Currently it is the residence of the ambassador of Sri Lanka. Number **18 Range**, the **Street residence**, is a W. E. Noffke design, built in 1920 for Colonel Douglas Richmond Street, commander of the Governor General's Footguards and director of the Ottawa Car Company. If you look at this carefully you can still detect Noffke's side porch, later filled in to provide extra interior space.

Now start to climb the rise to Laurier East. At the northwest section of the park, note Stephen Brathwaite's children's play area built in the summer of 1992. Brathwaite's concept features architectural remnants rescued from previously demolished Ottawa buildings. The art deco female heads hails from a Bank of Montreal. Brathwaite calls the sandbox "Strathcona's Folly," saying: "It's intended to provoke imagination and play. The theme is time – so children can imagine their future by seeing the ruins of the past."[13]

At the top of the hill is **453 Laurier**, **Le Cercle universitaire d'Ottawa**, the former **Munross House** of John Mather, lumber baron. The original structure is vastly altered, both in design and in function. Its second owner, Dr. Henry Ami, a geologist, had the castle-like turret added. W. E. Noffke's 1928 architectural drawings reveal he was hired to design the then-fashionable Tudor half-timber addition for the third owner, entrepreneur J. Ambrose O'Brien.

Head right on Laurier and then curve north on Charlotte. Number **285 Charlotte**, the **Embassy of the Russian Federation**, built in 1956, is another Noffke building. Originally dubbed "Stalinesque Brutalism" in style, it once presented a stolid, bleak image to the streetscape. However, during the summer of 1992 the façade was given a lift: the windows are now surrounded by exaggerated, inverted U-shaped mouldings of reflective glass. These pseudo-mouldings add sudden drama to the otherwise weary-looking building. According to Noffke historian Shannon Ricketts, the walls are "2 feet thick with a 14 inch concrete inner leaf, a 2 inch air gap in the middle and a 4 inch stone facing on the exterior."[14] Noffke's original plans show his signature urns on either side of the door.

Turn right (east) at Wilbrod to view **500 Wilbrod**, the **Andrew Fleck House**. This romantic Nepean sandstone house shows the irregular massing characteristic of the Queen Anne style. However, its rugged stonework of blond and red sandstone (sandblasted in 1992)

*View up the Rideau River, showing the footbridge to the Rideau Tennis Club from A. W. Fleck's gardens, Rideau St., Ottawa. Undated. NCC 061-53*

and its sturdy unadorned arches recall American architect H. H. Richardson's Romanesque Revival style so popular on the North American continent at the turn of the century.

Architect J. W. H. Watts designed this whimsical residence in 1903–05 for Andrew Fleck, the owner of the Vulcan Iron Works. English born, Watts came to Canada in 1874 when he was twenty-four years old. Here he designed a romantic mansion featuring a prominent castle-like rounded turret, a Spanish tile roof, and an offset entryway complete with stained-glass windows and a massive oak door. In their medieval romanticism – and exquisite craftsmanship – such features are reminiscent of the Arts and Crafts Movement. Detailing on the door includes the date "AD. 1901."

The home and its well-preserved carriage-house offers a strikingly whimsical contrast to the severe Russian Embassy you have just seen. Also known as the **Paterson House** after Senator Norman Paterson, its second owner, the house was sold in July 1992 to start its new life as a headquarters for an international transcendental meditation organization. Once again, active Sandy Hill residents intervened in the development of their community. An early proposal for renovating the house into Bed and Breakfast accommodation was rejected: insufficient parking spaces, potential noise and alcohol issues nixed this concept.

Walk to the end of Wilbrod for a splendid view of the Rideau River. If you wish, descend the rather steep stairs beside **550 Wilbrod**, **Wilbrod Place**, for another view of the river. **Cummings Bridge** spans the water on your left. First built of wood in 1836, the bridge is named after settler Charles Cummings. The city named a replacement bridge built in 1893 after Samuel Bingham and erected plaques proclaiming the "Bingham Bridge." But feisty Sandy Hill residents felt strongly about retaining the name, and someone tore the plaques down and threw them into the river.

Now backtrack on Wilbrod, keeping the 1980 solar-heated townhouses designed by Ecodomus to your right. The translucent fibreglass on the southern slopes of the roofs are solar panels. Basements are said to be 90 per cent filled with rocks for passive solar heat storage. Turn right (north) on Charlotte to walk along "apartment alley," between a series of high-density dwellings built in the early 1900s in response to the demand for more housing adjacent to downtown.

Turn left (west) on Daly and stop at the corner of Cobourg to admire **363–383 Daly, Philomène Terrace**. This is the oldest example of nineteenth-century stone row housing in Ottawa.

Antoine Robillard established a limestone quarry around 1840 on Montreal Road. Antoine worked for Thomas MacKay on the first eight entrance locks of the Rideau Canal, and also as a contractor for Rideau Hall. It was Antoine's son, Honoré, who built Philomène Terrace in 1874–75 in limestone for the quarry, and named it after his wife. Since then the six units have experienced successive alterations, owners and tenants. In 1888 verandahs were added to the three westernmost units, and in the 1890s the kitchens, originally in the basement, were relocated to three-storey rear brick additions.

Lumber merchant Isaac Moore lived in unit 363 prior to building his own residence at 240 Daly. Canadian poet Archibald Lampman lived in unit 369 between the years 1893 and 1896. His close friend, the poet Duncan Campbell Scott, observed that the house was cheap and damp. Nonetheless, Lampman was enthusiastic about the house as it was the first time he'd had a room of his own in which to write.

Stand back on the south side of Daly to appreciate the different front porches of the terrace. The Eastlake style of the two paired central wooden porches is named after Charles Locke Eastlake (1836–1906), who was an English interior designer, writer and architect. These porches feature beautifully ornate turning that gives a completely different ambiance to the Terrace than the plain squared, classically inspired porches of the two westernmost units. Notice their fanciful twists, turns and elaborate and delicate sunburst patterning with chamfered posts. In 1977–78 the City of Ottawa bought the two easternmost units and replaced their paired porches, but their attempt to emulate the Eastlake central four does not quite measure up. Notice, for example, how the central porches have turned supports, while the newer east porch supports are square. Together, the porches add a playful quality to Robillard's sturdy limestone structure, well matched by the picturesque pitched dormer windows.

Now turn right (north) on Cobourg and immediately left (west) on Besserer, named after the original property owner. Stop at **464 Besserer**, which **David Ewart** designed as his own home in 1873–74. It is utterly different from the fortress-like public buildings he designed. This house has no Scottish baronial overtones. Instead, it is an English Victorian Gothic cottage, which features prominent wooden brackets supporting its shallow, hat-like roof. The scrolled brackets

*464 Besserer, David Ewart's own home. The extension to the right was added later. Oct. 1991.* K. Fletcher

look as if they are melting. Trefoil-arched dormers protect Gothic window frames that are today almost obscured from view by modern, squared-off double-paned windows. Painted a deep blue, the trefoil detailing effectively contrasts with the off-white stucco of this home's sheer, otherwise unadorned walls. A projecting bay window, centre front of the main façade, adds interest, as does the bell-curved balustrading of the front porch.

Turn left (south) on Augusta, noting the use of modern but unusual exterior finish of board-and-batten, and the brick "cottages" framing the street. Number 226 was built in 1880 during Sandy Hill's building boom.

You now pass **336 Daly, Patterson House**, on the corner of Augusta, a pretty L-shaped Victorian Gothic cottage. This treasure was built in 1870 for Thomas Patterson, grocer. That year he procured a mortgage of $6,000 to build this charming vernacular home. The house has a cheerful and highly decorated exterior which exhibits much of the asymmetry popular with Victorians. Its yellow brick corner quoins are connected to the body of the house by a prominent yellow brick stringcourse, and the quoins are echoed in the differently shaped yellow brick window mouldings. Although the two roof gables are sharply peaked, here their similarity ends. One gable has a trefoil design, while the other, over the western wing, has extremely delicate wooden gingerbread trim (bargeboard). In 1906 architect Louis Fennings Taylor purchased the house and converted the interior to two apartments with a rear addition. Today its cottage ambiance is emphasized by the crowd of lilacs at the rear entry.

Number **286 Stewart, Pope House**, on the southwest corner at Augusta, is a completely different style. It is a Second Empire house, featuring tall, hipped wall dormers with peaked wooden caps. The house is unusual for its beautiful walled garden. It was built in 1875 for Christopher Grayburn. In 1907 Sir Joseph and Lady Pope moved in. Sir Joseph was private secretary to Prime Minister Sir John A. Macdonald. A verandah once stood where the brick addition is now located.

Across the street there is a plaque identifying the heritage architectural importance of Sandy Hill. Beside it is **245 Augusta**, built around 1870. It is a cream-coloured stucco Gothic cottage, the former home of Prime Minister Lester Pearson during the years 1947–54. Like Ewart's residence, the vernacular design of this house features wooden bargeboard beneath its eaves.

Continue down Augusta, what Coly Meredith once called a "treeless wasteland of mud," to Wilbrod. Turn right (west) and then immediately left (south) down a narrow laneway. The laneway first passes **400 Wilbrod**, a large brick mansion Coly Meredith designed in 1910, now the residence of the Ambassador of Brazil.

Next door is **395 Laurier East, Stadacona Hall**, the residence of the ambassador of Belgium. Originally built for lumber merchant John A. Cameron in 1871, the Gothic limestone cottage has undergone several transformations, including the addition of a garage built in 1945. Lilian Scott Desbarats, former Sandy Hill resident of nearby 274 Daly, observed the Camerons needed "a very big house because they had 11 children."[15]

Cameron rented to a series of tenants, including Sir John A. and Lady Agnes Macdonald in 1877–83. During their tenure peacocks strode the lawns, attracting curious children to the gates of the estate with their haunting cry and iridescent plumage. Explanations of its name vary. One story says that Sir John A. christened it Stadacona Hall after his Kingston political club; yet another claims that a later tenant, Hon. Joseph-Edouard Cauchon's wife, named it after the Iroquois name for the village that once stood where Quebec City now is.

Now turn right (west) on Laurier. Across from All Saints Church is **335, Laurier House**. Bequeathed by Lady Laurier to Prime Minister Mackenzie King in 1921, the home was originally built in 1878 for wealthy Ottawa jeweller John Leslie, whose shop was on Sparks Street. This house was the second on Laurier Avenue designed by James Mather: the first was Munross, now Le Cercle private club overlooking Strathcona Park. Prior to its many additions, Le Cercle was the mirror image of this home, having its bay on the left side, not on the right. Laurier House is now a museum. Go inside to enjoy its richly furnished interior, notably King's third-floor, wood-panelled library and study with its cozy fireplace.

This rambling house is a good example of the crossover of architectural styles. Its massing, with its five-sided wings and bays as well as its mansard roof identify it as Second Empire. However, details such as round-topped dormers and window mouldings are Italianate. The yellow brick of the exterior was traditionally referred to as "white brick." Noffke designed the wrap-around verandah in 1913 for Sir Wilfrid Laurier, who lived here from 1897 until his death in 1919.

*Laurier House in October 1902. Note the ironwork cresting, and the original porch predating Noffke's 1913 design for Sir Wilfrid Laurier. PAC-PA-8979*

*312 Laurier, Nov. 1991. Curved bay windows and projecting wings soften George Goodwin's massive brick mansion.* K. Fletcher

In 1922 Mackenzie King altered the interior space to suit his personal taste as well as public demands. The design by the firm of Sproatt & Rolph included a personal retreat for the prime minister on the top floor.

The blond brick of Laurier House is echoed in the sprawling thirty-three-room mansion now dwarfing its lot on the corner of Russell, **312 Laurier**, the **George Goodwin mansion**. The 1900 home features prominent rounded bays with symmetrical wings on its east and west sides. It has a fascinating past. Built for George Goodwin, a railway contractor, it is now the headquarters of the St. John Ambulance. During World War II, it served as the Kildare Annex, barracks for the Canadian Women's Army Corps. Six cells were built in the basement for those who transgressed strict army rules. The basement also contained a huge rainwater reservoir, reportedly the size of a swimming pool.

Continue along Laurier, past the ornate wrought-iron porch supports at number **301 Laurier** (opposite the Goodwin mansion). They are lovingly rendered, with highly detailed oak leaves and acorns, and adorn an otherwise ordinary gabled home.

*16 Sweetland, Nov. 1991. Brick corner quoins, delicate wrought-iron balconies and polychromatic brickwork enliven this investment flat-top.* K. Fletcher

*The iron gate at 16 Sweetland. Nov. 1991. K. Fletcher*

*24–34 Sweetland. Nov. 1991.* K. Fletcher

Turn left (south) on Sweetland, past **16 Sweetland**. Built in 1886, this brick flat-top apartment building is defined by a wrought-iron fence. Its gate announces "J. Harry, 1886."

Pass **24–34 Sweetland**, beautiful brick row houses, which feature rounded false parapet gables projecting above their flat-topped roofs. Note the detailed dentil cornice and bracket supports. Ornate porches with turned posts and windows framed by arched brick voussoirs create an elegant façade to the street. Inset porch entryways are shared, but beautifully arched tongue-and-groove dividers provide a degree of privacy. The row houses at **38–48 Sweetland** feature highly detailed spooling on their front porches.

Dr. John Sweetland, sheriff of Carleton County in 1867, is remembered in the name of the street you are now exploring. Near the top of the hill is **62 Sweetland**. Built in 1895, the City has awarded it heritage designation as a superb example of a nineteenth-century home. Built for Sarah and Andrew Mitrow, the steeply gabled, L-shaped red brick home has an ornamental verandah with scrolled and turned woodwork. Note the projecting finial at the peak of the home's front-end gable.

Now turn right (west) on Osgoode. At the corner of Osgoode and Henderson Streets is the **École Francojeunesse**. Strong horizontal

*École Francojeunesse. Contrasting colours enliven the school's façade. Nov. 1991.*
K. Fletcher

lines are emphasized by the contrast between rough-hewn grey lime-stone layers and the rich red brick façade. Highly detailed terracotta capitals with a typically Romanesque organic motif adorn either side of the generously arched entryway on Osgoode. This detailing is characteristic of the solid Romanesque Revival architectural style so popular for late nineteenth-century schools. Architectural mates to this school include First Avenue and Mutchmor schools (*see* Glebe walk).

In order to get a close-up look of a now-rare pressed-tin façade to a building, take just a few steps south to see **93 Henderson**. Barely hanging on to life, this old garage's front façade has a different pattern from that on its southern side.

Continue along Osgoode until you reach King Edward. You are now facing the entryway to the **University of Ottawa**. Its post-modern residences form a visual continuum south down the western façade of King Edward Avenue.

The tall tower you can see to your far left forms a stylized cross. It is a "modern heritage" landmark of Ottawa which symbolically recalls the university's 1848 founding by Bishop Guigues as the Collège de Bytown (*see* Sussex walk). The tower marks the southern-most extent of the main campus and is actually a chimney for the heating plant of the university. In 1972 Murray & Murray, with associate architect Louis Lapierre, won an award for this innovative design.

Now take a few steps to your left on King Edward, and then an almost immediate right, to enter the walkway through the **Brooks residence**, at **620–622 King Edward**. Here the quarters for married students feature a colourful children's playground.

At the end of this short walkway is Louis Pasteur Private. The word "private" here means that this street is not maintained or owned by the City. Take a seat and soak in the atmosphere of the university. A campus has a life of its own, being a city within a city, and the challenge for the designer is considerable. Inexpensive yet functional residences for faculty and students are mandatory; well-lit walkways safe for students who are burning the midnight oil must be land-scaped; and visually stimulating yet functional, cost-effective struc-tures such as laboratories and libraries that balance communal areas with private study carrels must be designed. Between the years 1969–71 a master plan for the university was devised by the architects Martineau, Lapierre, and Murray & Murray Associates.

*Montpetit Hall, University of Ottawa: Brutalist lines present smooth, sheer walls and regularly spaced, smoked-glass windows. Nov. 1991. K. Fletcher*

At Louis Pasteur turn left and then immediately right onto University Private. Note the daringly angled planes of the 1973 **Montpetit Hall's** smoked glass windows. Stay on University Private as it turns right (north), and pass the twin brick highrise residences of **Marchand Hall** and **Stanton Hall** before turning left again on Calixa-Lavalée (named for the composer of Canada's National Anthem) and then right alongside the Transitway, which hurtles buses from Highway 417 to the city centre. From here you get a splendid view of the Rideau Canal and Centre Town, of the juxtaposition of the old Cartier Square Drill Hall, the copper châteauesque peaks of the Lord Elgin Hotel (*see* Canal walk), and the shining silver orb atop the 1991 World Exchange Plaza.

Continue alongside the Transitway. Directly ahead of you is the flamboyant 1883 **Odell House** at **180 Waller.** Horace C. Odell, brick mason and brickyard owner, built the house as a wedding gift for his son Clarence. It exhibits many features of the Second Empire style so popular in the late 1800s. Incorporated into the jaunty tower and mansard roof are round-headed dormer windows. The first-floor windows are framed by draped hood mouldings with prominent keystones. There are two entryways to the home: one has a lovely wishbone gable atop its porch; the other is centred in an Italianate

*180 Waller. Horace C. Odell's Second Empire present to his son Clarence. Nov. 1991. E. Fletcher*

tower, the inset windows in its double-door making it a gracious entry.

Perched today between Waller, the Transitway and Laurier East, the home has forever lost its original garden setting. But its colourful whimsy adds a touch of glamour to the busy campus. The University of Ottawa bought it in the 1970s.

Numbers **183–173 Waller** are grey-painted former homes now owned by the university, housing faculty offices. At least one second-floor office boasts its original fireplace framed by a wooden mantle-piece with inset tiles depicting farm animals.

Across from 180 Waller is **Simard Hall**, the **Arts Faculty** (1955), sporting features inspired by Art Deco. Stylized vertically-fluted pilasters simulate classical pillars on either side of the entryway. The doorway is highlighted by a façade of windows extending the full four storeys, supported by exposed aluminum framing with "lamps of learning" on either side. Look at the metalwork detailing of the window for another stylized cross.

Continue to the corner of Waller and Laurier East. To your left (northwest) you can see the austere limestone wall of the old jail, where Patrick Whelan was hung February 11, 1869, for the assassination of Thomas D'Arcy McGee. His was the last public hanging in Canada. As was usual for such macabre spectacles, Whelan's hanging drew thousands of spectators who came by horse-drawn sleigh, snowshoe and foot from even remote rural locations.

Directly to your right (northeast) is the splendid rear view of the classical, European-looking **Tabaret Hall, 550 Cumberland**. Turn right on Laurier East and walk on the north side to the grassy park in front of Tabaret Hall. From the park you can best see the towering Ionic columns supporting the massive central dome of the building. A plaque just inside the Laurier entrance describes the 1903 destruction of the original building by fire. Tabaret Hall was designed by New York architect Count A. O. Von Herbulis in 1904–05 in the Beaux-Arts Classical style because it captures the notion of the university as a temple of learning.

Return to Laurier. At the corner of Laurier and Cumberland streets is **591 Laurier, Sacre Coeur Church**. Built in 1981, it replaced the Neo-

*Rear view of Tabaret Hall. Nov. 1991. K. Fletcher*

Gothic limestone church that burned down on November 24, 1978. Today's Sacre Coeur is open at noon for mass and is well worth seeing inside. The open interior space is warmed by natural and artificial lighting, and the sanctuary and sacristy have an air of approachability uncommon in older churches. The ceiling volumes are filled with a criss-cross of metal trusses, which relieve the austerity of the textured limestone walls. Honey-coloured oak pews are angled, seeming to invite the congregation to take full part in the service.

Opposite the church is **151 Laurier, St. Joseph's Rectory**. It is reminiscent of the California Mission style with its smooth white stucco surface and contrasting vermilion highlights. However, some details are inconsistent with California Mission, including its oriel rounded bay windows. Nonetheless, it provides a refreshingly different architectural motif to this hectic corner.

Continue east along Laurier until you reach King Edward. Turn left (north).

Number **519–525 King Edward, Martin Terrace**, is named after Daniel Martin, a grocer who developed this property with his wife, Isabella. These four townhouses, designed by German architect Adam Harvey in 1903, are one of Ottawa's best-loved heritage sites.

*151 Laurier. Nov. 1991.* K. Fletcher

*Martin Terrace. Porthole windows, two "half-timbered" gables and two differently-capped turrets add whimsy to King Edward. Oct. 1991. K. Fletcher*

In his design, Harvey catered to the Victorian taste for asymmetrical groupings of dissimilar parts. The wrought-iron fence defining the property edge provides continuity and relief to Harvey's juxtaposition of rounded and peaked turrets, porthole and peaked dormer windows, in the mansard roof. Coly Meredith commented that fences such as these kept early residents' wandering livestock at bay: "Nearly everyone tried to grow their own vegetables and many kept a cow but frequently the cow got lost or some stray cow or horse would get in and eat and trample the garden."[16]

Adjacent to Martin Terrace are numbers **515–517 King Edward** (1895) and, built roughly two years later, numbers **503–509, Linden Terrace**. Many residents of the area were senior civil servants who urgently required housing in the boom years following Confederation.

At Wilbrod, turn left for a moment to see **210 Wilbrod, St. Paul's Evangelical Church**, designed in 1888 by Adam Harvey, and also to see **209 Wilbrod, W. E. Noffke's** first home, which he designed in 1904 for himself and his wife, Ida. Noffke attended St. Paul's and apprenticed with its architect, Adam Harvey.

Return to King Edward and continue north to Daly, where you will find the second Anglican parish of Ottawa, the **Church of St. Alban's the Martyr** (1867–77), the first church in Canada to offer its congregation free seats. It was built to accommodate part of the congregation of the first Anglican church of Ottawa, Christ Church Cathedral, which was bursting at the seams (*see* Parliament walk). After Thomas Fuller's design had been approved, and after excavation had commenced, workers discovered an unwelcome pit of unstable sand, a natural intrusion in the clay subsoil.

Fuller's design could not be built and he withdrew it, recommending that a student of his, architect King Arnoldi, complete the church. Arnoldi was hired and retained much of Fuller's plans, except for the tall spire which could not be supported by the unstable foundation. Although St. Alban's opened in 1867 it took ten more years to complete. Many political figures joined the congregation, including Sir John A. Macdonald, Sir Charles Tupper, Sir Alexander Campbell, and Viscount Monck, the first governor general of Canada. Sir John walked to the church from nearby Stadacona Hall, as did Campbell from his residence at Varin Row on Daly.

This church and St. Bartholomew's (*see* New Edinburgh walk) share medieval, early English Gothic stylistic details. However, perhaps because of its gentler, treed setting, "St. Bart's" is less austere than this church, perched here on the busy street. St. Alban's has a steep gabled roof with two cross gables, and features prominent buttress supports. Note the slim open belfry resembling an arrowhead,

*149 Daly with 157–159 Daly to the rear. Nov. 1991.* K. Fletcher

which has a tall wrought-iron pinnacle. It is visually connected to St. Alban's easternmost end gable by iron cresting. Look for the trefoil, quatrefoil and cinquefoil motifs in the ornate window tracery.

Before crossing King Edward look at **149 Daly**, the **Besserer House**, on the northeast corner of King Edward. This 1844 residence was the home of Théodore Besserer, the brother of Sandy Hill's original landowner, Louis. It is strategically located on the ridge of Sandy Hill, overlooking Lowertown, which Colonel By described in 1831 as being "a large swamp." The height undoubtedly afforded Besserer and his wife some relief from the smell of Sandy Hill drains and the dust of its summer roads.

The house is a Georgian design of cut limestone. You can still see the square base of the original widow's walk atop the roof – what a splendid view it must have had! The classical balance of the façade is curiously skewed on the second storey by a fourth horizontal window set between the upper left windows. Otherwise, symmetry is maintained by the two end chimneys and half-circle dormer windows inset into the roof.

Cross King Edward to walk east on Daly to see a variety of intriguing residences. Number **157–159 Daly** is a whimsical potpourri of effects, including a grey tin roof with matching painted brick and circular turret. Georgian-inspired **161 Daly** was built in 1872 by the first Anglican bishop of Ottawa, John Travers Lewis. Its striking corner quoins and horizontal stringcourses of smooth cut stone contrast dramatically with the rough-cut limestone façade. Number **185 Daly, McGee's Inn**, was owned by John J. McGee, half brother to the famous orator, ill-fated Thomas D'Arcy McGee.

Number **192 Daly** sports a plaque identifying it as built in 1893 for John Roberts Allen, an Ottawa businessman. The house's exuberance is characteristic of the Queen Anne style. It features a rounded porch, terracotta capitals, delicate iron cresting atop the porch and projecting bay window, and turned wooden detailing beneath sharply gabled eaves. In the late 1930s the Japanese ambassador Mr. Tokugawa was renting the premises. It became the Japanese Legation until Pearl Harbour was attacked on December 7, 1941. In her published memoirs, Lilian Desbarats of Sandy Hill reported that after war was declared the RCMP patrolled 192 Daly on a twenty-four-hour basis.

Numbers **199–205 Daly** are investment townhouses built around 1870 for William McFarlane. During the 1860s and 1870s brick became a popular building material. The regular features of the building such as evenly spaced windows and dormers are artistically offset by the

*199–205 Daly. Beautifully restored units feature contrasting mouldings above each window. Oct. 1991.* K. Fletcher

dramatically contrasting corner quoins and window mouldings. Note the wooden bracket supports beneath its overhanging eaves. Other investment properties on this block include **208–214 Daly** and **202–204**, which have gabled roofs with dormers and raised firewalls.

Number **274 Daly** was built around 1865 and in 1867 became the residence of **Sir Charles Tupper**, one of the fathers of Confederation. By 1874 it was home to **Sir Richard W. Scott**, once secretary of state, senator, mayor of Ottawa and, earlier, one of the principal lobbyists promoting Ottawa as capital. His daughter Lilian – who married neighbour George Desbarats – observed in her memoirs of Sandy Hill, *Recollections*, that "Tupper was a doctor and for years after in a pile of ashes at the back of the house we children were so pleased to find medicine bottles of all shapes and sizes." It was here at 274 that Lilian worried about storing her seventy-five-pound wedding cake in the basement, terrified that the rats would "eat it all up."

Number **309–311 Daly**, **Winterholme**, now called the **Chapel Court Apartments**, was built for George Desbarats, Canada's first Queen's Printer. The property originally belonged to Richard Scott, who advised Desbarats that building a home in Sandy Hill would be just the thing – and that, coincidentally, *he* owned the perfect spot. The rambling limestone home, complete with conservatory, was erected in 1868. It used to front upon Besserer with a gracious, treed circular drive leading to its front door.

Ottawa politics of the day conspired against the printer. Desbarat's press was at the corner of Sparks where Thomas D'Arcy McGee was assassinated. Because Desbarats erected a plaque to McGee's memory on his building, Fenians threatened to destroy his business. The building was then gutted by fire. Desbarats decided he'd had enough of Ottawa. He sold his beautiful house to Sir Sanford Fleming and returned to Montreal. In her memoirs, Lilian Desbarats recalled the conservatory: "It was the most fascinating place to sit out dances. The tropical scents and exotic plants were delightful. There was an orange tree, I remember, with golden fruit handing from the branches. Sir Sanford took the conservatory down and made a vast room instead. This room proved very useful when the house was given over a convalescent home for invalid soldiers, coming home during and after World War I."

When the home was divided into apartments in 1925, the dramatic Besserer entry was removed. During the alterations, a large bay window that Prime Minister Mackenzie King admired was purchased by him and dismantled. He removed it to Kingsmere in Gatineau Park, where it is part of his well-known collections of "ruins." Forever gone, too, is the lovely rose garden, Sir Sandford's pride and joy.

Before turning right on Chapel, walk a few steps farther east on Daly to view number **315 Daly**, built around 1861 for Mr. Duncan Graham. A stone house, it originally cost $4,000 and boasted an observatory and a verandah. The original symmetry of the house is broken by the eastern extension done by Cecil Burgess (drawings dated May, 1949). The joinery in the masonry and also in the eaves and roofline are visible. At its rear is a brick addition, similar to that of Philomène Terrace, which was added at the turn of the century. The home is now a housing co-op.

Now backtrack to turn left (south) on Chapel, viewing in passing **229 Chapel** the **Plummer**, or **Toller, House**, yet another large Victorian Gothic brick home built in 1875 for J. H. Plummer, manager of the Bank of Commerce. It was purchased in 1877 by Télesphore Fournier, politician, journalist, lawyer, member of the Supreme Court who was both minister of revenue and of justice in mid-1870. In 1882 the house was purchased by Lieutenant-Colonel Frederick Toller who served as comptroller of the Dominion currency for 29 years. The house passed to another politician, Louis Philippe Brodeur, until 1931, when Les Soeurs Blanche D'Afrique, a French order of Nuns, took over.

They ran a school and residence here for many years. Present owner Eric Cohen initially proposed using the home as a shelter for homeless women – but in 1991 Sandy Hill residents successfully opposed the plan, getting the support of the Ontario Municipal Board (OMB). Today, Cohen's fall-back position is that he might convert the once lovely single family residence into a rooming house, possibly for forty-two tenants. Once again Sandy Hill residents have taken their opposition to the OMB. As of February 1993, their ruling has not been declared.

Architects Horsey and Sheard designed Toller House. *The Ottawa Citizen* of December 6, 1875 reported on its exquisite interior: "The

*229 Goulburn. Oct. 1991.* K. Fletcher

hall floor is constructed of walnut and ash strips. The parlor, dining room and library are spacious and lofty. The upper flats are utilized for bedrooms, dressing and bathrooms, and are supplied with hot and cold water. The whole building is heated with hot air. It cost about $9,000. "

Continue south along Chapel to Somerset Street East. Turn left (east) and then right onto Goulburn. Climb the hill.

On your left you pass **229 Goulburn**. This colourfully painted now-uncommon clapboard home on a rough-cut limestone base is pleasantly sited on a roomy, treed lot.

Number **265 Goulburn** is one of Ottawa's few modernist homes, a composition of strongly defined horizontal bands. The flat roof, trimmed in grey with its ever-so-slightly protruding chimney is echoed by the dramatic stringcourse above the second-storey windows. The linear motif is further emphasized by the canopy above the front door, the careful placement of the repeated window motifs, and also by the linear pattern made by the rusticated base. Note the balanced upper and lower windows located on the left corner of the home. Corner windows maximized light penetration of the interior, and they have become a cliché of modernist design.

Turn left on Mann. Ahead, bordering the Queensway, are a collection of rectangular 1960s and 1990s post-modern CMHC and City of

*265 Goulburn is a rare residential example of the modernist style. Oct. 1991.* K. Fletcher

*245 Range, a cottage overlooking the Rideau. Oct. 1991.* K. Fletcher

Ottawa units, public housing that provides high density living. The old Mann Avenue arena to your west used to be a brickyard.

Head left (north) on Range Road. Note **245 Range**, the **Meredith House**, perched atop a hill with a splendid view of the river. It is a charming, simple cottage designed by Coly Meredith in 1920 for himself and his wife, Aldie. Of it he wrote: "In January 1920 Aldie and I skied over to the end of Range Road ... At that time there was nothing but an open field from the Rideau River to Blackburn Avenue and from Templeton to Mann Avenue with the exception of the Nurses' Residence by the Hospital, there were no roads except on the city maps, and sewers and water were put in later. We decided to take the lot ... and build a small house. ... As the South end extended over the Hillside little excavation was required, this is the reason that part of the basement is built in masonry, the rest of the foundation was built later."[17]

Today the house retains its charming Normandy country cottage appeal, with its massive chimney, dramatic roofline of low-slung flaring eaves and its smooth plastered walls.

Continue north along Range. Number **85 Range**, the **Sandringham Apartments**, are on your right, on the site of the old Strathcona Hospital. This was torn down in the early 1950s, when the East Lawn pavilion of the Civic Hospital opened on Carling Avenue.

*Sandringham Apartments. Oct. 1991.* K. Fletcher

*68 Range. Oct. 1991.* K. Fletcher

The Sandringham was designed by architect Peter Dickinson, who came to Canada in 1950 from Britain. It is one of the twin modernist blocks he originally intended for the site. Its monolithic structure is relieved by his signature flaring entrance canopy, and also by the contrast of glass, brick and open space created by the recessed balconies.

Farther north is **68 Range**. The horizontal planes and smooth surfaces of this modest house are similar to its modernist companion at 265 Goulburn. Here, however, curves and a stepped-back plan add extra interest. The curves of the doorway canopy are repeated in the front plant containers and the steps leading to the side entrance.

You are soon back at Somerset. But before you return to your car, turn left and walk a block to view **346 Somerset**, the **Francis Sullivan House**. Designed in 1914, the house shows the influence of Frank Lloyd Wright's Prairie School in its shallow roof and projecting eaves. The blue-painted borders surrounding the highly decorative, multi-paned windows, and the paned horizontal bands encircling the textured stucco façade lend the house a jaunty mood. Sullivan added such decorative touches to his own home as the Japanese screen, or grillwork, shielding the front entry.

Backtrack to your car at Strathcona Park.

*346 Somerset East, the Francis Sullivan home. Oct. 1991.* K. Fletcher

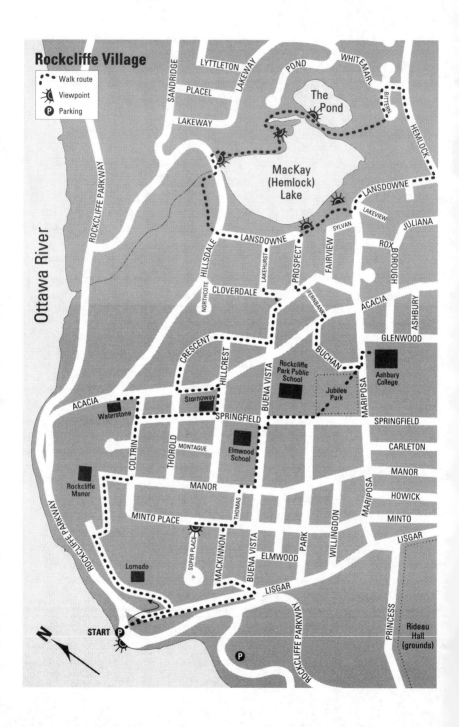

# Rockcliffe Village

## History

In 1885, when Lowertown was bustling with activity and after the City of Ottawa was beginning to annex its suburbs, the area known as Rockcliffe remained remote countryside. Ten years later, in August 1895, Thomas Coltrin Keefer's electric streetcar line was opened between Main Street, New Edinburgh, and Rockcliffe Park. Now Ottawans could easily travel to a new recreation venue to enjoy in their hard-earned leisure time. Labourers, domestics and shop clerks could never hope to purchase land – nor could they dream of heading to a summer cottage in the Gatineau Hills. Instead, in ever-increasing numbers, they visited Rockcliffe Park.

*Rockcliffe Park streetcar.* NCC 172-140

Rockcliffe Park was essentially the creation of Thomas Coltrin Keefer, son-in-law to Thomas MacKay, contractor of the Rideau Canal. When MacKay died in 1855 at Rideau Hall, he left a significant estate. T. C. Keefer took over the management of the estate. In 1864 he had a map drawn to advertise the sale of "Park, Villa, and Village Lots" of the MacKay Estate.

He was an astute businessman. Keefer purchased the land fronting the river north of Lisgar Road, realizing it could become invaluable parkland – and a useful buffer between Rideau Hall and the development of Rockcliffe Village. He sold what is now Rockcliffe Park to the City for $34,000 on July 27, 1897. In 1904 the City arranged a fifteen year lease with the OIC for its maintenance. Today it is managed by the NCC.

Keefer's 1864 map shows the "Rideau Hall Domain" and several other features of Rockcliffe Village. A deposit of white marl east of Hemlock Lake (now known as MacKay Lake) that Thomas Clark later used for his 1872 brickworks is shown. Also depicted is "Beaver Meadow," today's Beechwood shopping district. The map shows two residences in Rockcliffe: MacKay's Elmdale farm, now the site of Elmwood girls school, and Birkenfels, a stone dwelling. Roads such as Buena Vista were yet unnamed: it appears as an access route past the farm (Elmwood) to the fishing haven of Hemlock Lake.

Sales of MacKay estate lots were not brisk. During his tenure as governor general at Rideau Hall from 1867–68, Lord Monck could not abide the dust, mud and potholes of Sussex Drive connecting Rideau Hall to his East Block office. Despite his access to the most luxurious conveyances of the day, he deplored the long drive along Sussex. Instead, he insisted upon having at his personal disposal a navy ship, which was docked at Governor's Bay.

If New Edinburgh's Government House was considered too far away, Rockcliffe was even more remote. Even by 1925, early resident Asconi J. Major and his family decided to sell Stornoway, because commuting to their Lowertown business was too onerous. Population figures for the development of the village are revealing. The Rockcliffe of 1890 had only twelve households, in 1900 there were thirty, and by 1914 sixty, mostly clustered around Lisgar Road. By 1926, 150 fifty-foot lots had been laid out between Mariposa and Maple Lane, west of Ashbury, but only twenty had sold. East of Hemlock Lake was a sandy, poorly drained area.

All through these years, the park remained a popular recreation area, summer and winter. Governor General Lord Lorne installed an

TOBOGGANNING AT GOV-
ERNMENT HOUSE.

*The toboggan run. Rideau Hall visible at rear.* NCC 172

astonishing toboggan run, lit by a railway engine headlight, that
started at Rideau Hall, crossed the present Driveway and cut down
the steep cliffs onto the ice of Governor's Bay.

At the turn of the century skiing became the rage. Lord Frederick Hamilton introduced the sport to Ottawa: "In January 1887, I brought my Russian skis to Ottawa, the very first pair that had ever been seen in the New World. I coasted down hills on them amidst universal jeers; everyone declared they were quite unsuitable to the Canadian conditions."[18]

By 1910 the Ottawa Ski Club had erected "Suicide Hill" in Rockcliffe Park, a ski jump 128 feet high that so captured the imagination of Ottawans that thousands lined the jump on Saturdays – and even Sundays – to watch the spectacle. Lady Kingsmill, wife of Admiral Kingsmill, whose residence we view later (8 Crescent), sold coffee and sandwiches to the enthusiastic crowds watching the likes of club president Joe Morin sailing through the air on skis.

Tobogganing, snowshoeing, skiing, skating and sleighing – all these winter pastimes encouraged residents and visitors alike to enjoy the beautiful scenery of Rockcliffe Park. But what of the first residences?

Thomas MacKay's first neighbour was Duncan Reynier MacNab, another Scot, who started to build his Regency style stone house, Rockcliffe Manor, in 1839. MacNab was quartermaster with Colonel By's regiment. History suggests a rivalry between MacNab and MacKay, with the former hoping to out-shine MacKay's Castle with the erection of a bigger, more expansive home. However, MacNab died at age thirty-six before occupying his house.

By this time, MacKay had completed Birkenfels, another gracious stone home close to his Rideau Hall property. After MacKay's death in 1855, Thomas Coltrin Keefer purchased Rockcliffe Manor in the late 1860s for Thomas MacKay's widow, the former Anne Crichton. Under the conditions of managing the MacKay estate, Keefer and his first wife, Elizabeth (Thomas MacKay's youngest daughter), moved into Birkenfels.

More residents came to Rockcliffe, including the Short family from England. Visible on Keefer's map of 1864, Elmdale farm was well situated to provide produce, hay and cattle for New Edinburgh's and Rockcliffe's growing population. Thomas Short rented the farm for many years. As a lad, Tom's son Sam held various jobs, including being Lord Dufferin's page and – after being dismissed from his vice-regal functions – he became a cow-boy, watching over upwards of 600 cows that pastured in Rockcliffe's woods and meadows. The fee for grazing was $1.00 per month per cow; Sam received a small percentage of the take.

By the year 1889, Sam had purchased one-and-a-half acres at Buena Vista and Springfield Roads, built a home and developed one of the capital's most lovely gardens. He now worked at the Ottawa Post Office, and managed to get there even in the winter despite the distance of more than a country mile. "When there was not even a sleigh mark, young Short donned his snowshoes and broke trail to St. Patrick's bridge. Traversing Sussex Street he noticed the horse-drawn cabin sleighs of the street railway bouncing through drifts and dipping over the waves of snow ridges into the hollows or "cahoots" formed by Ottawa's first street transportation system. Then in the spring break-up he got to the city by laying stones and jumping from one to the other to cross the creek running from Lindenlea. When the Shorts bought a new piano, in those years when there was plenty of time in the Village, with taxes at $5 per year, it took 10 days to get delivery of the piano from Ottawa, and then the last mile was by stone-boat, the half-ton truck of that day."[19]

The turn of the century saw the extension of Rockcliffe Park. "The Coming National Park at Rockcliffe" was big news in the Ottawa papers, including *The Evening Journal* of January 24, 1903, which

*Rockcliffe Park.* NCC 061-3

announced the OIC's intention to "make a monster pleasure ground for the capital. Nearly half a million dollars to be spent in work of beautifying the district beyond the City's present park."

When development of Sandy Hill's Strathcona Park precluded that neighbourhood's usefulness as the Dominion Rifle Range, the Rifle Association moved to a northern extension of Rockcliffe Park. So began this area's involvement with the Canadian military. Today the area once used by the 43rd Duke of Connaught's Rifles is the RCMP stables.

Enclosed on all sides by parklands, the Village of Rockcliffe was insulated from haphazard development. Thomas Coltrin Keefer, who died in 1915, successfully laid the groundwork for the planned, gradual growth of the MacKay Estate. Large lot sizes and broad streets, and the area's natural features, which include high limestone cliffs overlooking the Ottawa River, and wooded hillsides surrounding Hemlock Lake, all conspired to produce an environment of great beauty.

Today Rockcliffe Village has retained its independence status despite two modern attempts at annexation. The first, in 1977, came when the Mayo Report recommended it become part of Vanier. A year later, the City of Ottawa proposed annexation. Residents rallied and the Villagers won their battle for independent status. In 1992–93, villagers were again outraged by Graeme Kirby's study proposing a regional government which would absorb Rockcliffe Village.

## Neighbourhood Styles

Gracious estates, sweeping lawns and treed lots characterize Rockcliffe Village. The absence of sidewalks lends intimacy to any stroll around the village. Cars and bicycles, dogs and pedestrians share the road. Village bylaws of the 1920s restricted all building to single family dwellings. There are no intrusive apartment buildings, no corner stores, no restaurants to sully the carefully preserved landscape of quiet residences. In fact, the only break to the landscape of designer homes are the three schools nestled at the centre of the village: Ashbury College, Elmwood and Rockcliffe Park Public School. The schools surround what is known as the Village Square. Adjacent to the last school is the police station.

Many of the grand old homes are too large for today's families. Gardeners and domestic staff are beyond most people's means, even in well-heeled Rockcliffe. As a result, most of the large estates are now embassy properties. Although this has some drawbacks for the community, the benefits outweigh most of them, for diplomatic missions enjoy substantially more funding than do private persons, enabling the grand mansions to be looked after as they were originally intended. One has only to consider such once-beautiful homes as Sir Sandford Fleming's 1868 Winterholme – now irretrievably altered as the multi-unit, forlorn Chapel Court Apartments in Sandy Hill – to realize how quickly a building can lose its soul. However, patrolling security guards, "hidden" cameras and the crushing congestion of embassy traffic during a midday soirée are undeniably disturbing.

Because it attracted the wealthy, Rockcliffe Village is a repository of fashionable architectural trends. Here you find the legacy of Thomas Coltrin Keefer through the work of his architect grandson Allan Keefer, who designed many period style houses as well as Ashbury College. Omnipresent Ottawa architect W. E. Noffke's work is here too, as are the more avant-garde designs of award-winning Hart Massey. Today immense and often sadly ostentatious infill and the severing of the few remaining large estates such as Birkenfels, are destroying the pastoral character of the village. Yet the splendid natural setting of Rockcliffe Park remains.

Village residents fought long and hard to establish the 1970s conservation zone to preserve the precious habitats of MacKay Lake (Hemlock Lake) and the Pond. It remains to be seen if infill developments such as Bittern Court on the Pond, and sprawling homes such as 700 Hillside, beside the lake, will obliterate this achievement.

### Walk Tips

8 km; 4 hours.
The walk starts at the lookout over the Ottawa River. There are a few parking spaces here. Please note that although it is blocked off in winter, alternate parking spaces are available at the old bandshell, situated to the west of this lookout. There are also washroom facilities here that are usually open in summer. There are no restaurants, corner stores or gas stations in Rockcliffe Village itself.

Rockcliffe teems with embassy residences so security is prominent. There are no sidewalks to amble; remember to watch for cars as you walk. Please respect private property, particularly around MacKay Lake, the Pond and along "the Dog Walk," where gardens cascade down the sloped embankment to the water's edge, but the docks are private grounds.

## The Walk

Park your car at the Rockcliffe lookout over the Ottawa River built in 1923 by the Federal District Commission. The view north, of Pointe Gatineau, is of the homes hugging the waterfront and of the spires of St. François de Sales church.

The lookout is located east of the Ottawa Electric Railway Company's bandshell and amusement park. Here Ottawans who took the tram to escape the city for an afternoon were entertained by brass bands. Below you is the spot where Seguin's ferry landed honeymooners from "the other side" to revel in strains of such favourites as "Daisy, Daisy, Give Me Your Answer Do."

With the Ottawa River at your back, turn left and walk a few paces to Lisgar Road (*see* map: there is no road sign here). Opposite you will notice a smaller version of Rockcliffe Park's lookout. This Japanese pagoda-like shelter marks one of the old private entries to the electric streetcar line used by the people of Rockcliffe Village who lived on top of the craggy outcrop of rock before you. There is some debate as to how Rockcliffe got its name, but the elevation from the river to the top of the cliffs above you is the probable derivation.

Turn right along Lisgar, towards the pine knoll. After about thirty metres you will note a road heading sharply left, looping in a hairpin turn to the top of the hill. This is the roadway that ascends the cliff beside the U.S. ambassador's residence.

*Lornado, home of the U.S. Ambassador.* NCC 230

This house is **500 Lisgar Road, Lornado**, the former home of Warren Y. Soper, owner of the Ottawa Electric Railway Company with partner Thomas Ahearn. Lornado is situated on land that was once part of the original Birkenfels estate. Birkenfels itself is the stone home built by Thomas MacKay. The Birkenfels property was severed, and Soper purchased it from the MacKay estate in 1890. In 1908, Soper built this stone "cottage," which he called Lornado, after the heroine of the romantic novel *Lorna Doone*. Soper rented Birkenfels to military families and used Lornado as his home. After his wife died in 1931, the Lornado portion of the estate was bought by the U.S. Embassy and became the residence to successive U.S. ambassadors.

Lornado is a solid-looking mansion, regally placed above the cliffs on its expansive lawns – hardly what anyone today would term a cottage. As you climb the hill, its stone wall rises above you on your right like a medieval castle's battlements. It even has small vertical openings reminiscent of a castle's slots for archers. Lornado, which has a widow's walk atop its flattened roof, is the first of many Rockcliffe houses that has a magnificent view of the Ottawa River valley.

Continue up the driveway until you reach Manor Avenue. The road turns sharply right at **46 Manor, Coltrin Lodge**, designed by Allan Keefer when he was about eighteen years old. This is the first of the prolific architect's designs that we see on this walk. Keefer designed the house for his older sister, who lived here until 1943 when she sold to W. D. Mathers, assistant undersecretary of state for external affairs. Mathers greatly altered the original home.

On the left as the road curves east, lies **740 Manor, Marchmont**, the Indonesian ambassador's residence. Its main entry is marked by large Florentine gateposts.

Now continue on Manor. You pass a ranch-style house looking peculiarly squashed by its dark-shingled, mansard-style roof.

Next door is **725 Manor**, a residence designed by architect Barry Hobin, built in 1992–93. Here in Rockcliffe, it is a refreshing interpretation of Frank Lloyd Wright's Prairie Style motif. Horizontal bands of windows that wrap around upper storey corners must afford spectacular views of the private gardens of Rockcliffe Manor, the Ottawa River and the Gatineau Hills. Note the detailing of the door, reminiscent of Glasgow architect Charles Rennie Mackintosh's designs.

Continue to **724 Manor, Rockcliffe Manor House**, now the **Apostolic Nunciate**, where the Pope's Vatican representative to

*Rockcliffe Manor House, now the Apostolic Nunciate, as seen through the gateway.* NCC 230-74

Canada lives. This historic house is the Rockcliffe's answer to Rideau Hall. The original Regency style stone cottage with surrounding verandahs was built by Duncan Reynier MacNab. As mentioned earlier, MacNab died before completing the cottage, which featured imposing chimneys and gables. Also included in the initial design was a Georgian entry with French doors, and a covered verandah once surrounded the home on three sides. Today the house is hardly a Regency cottage, but rather a splendid home in the style of eighteenth-century French manor houses.

This house has been home to several prominent Ottawans. MacNab's death and the leasing in 1865 of Rideau Hall as Lord Monck's vice-regal residence prompted T. C. Keefer, as manager of the MacKay Estate, to purchase Manor House for MacKay's widow, Anne. Upon her death, Keefer moved in here with his wife, Annie (daughter of Anne and Thomas MacKay). Keefer substantially altered the home by adding Victorian gables with dormers and a beautifully curved bargeboard trim. After Keefer died in 1915, his son Charles Keefer lived here for a few years, then rented it until 1929, when it was sold to Canada's first female senator, Cairine Wilson, and her husband, Norman Wilson.

Cairine Wilson hired Boston architect J. W. Ames to completely re-do the home. The sole reminder of MacNab's original house is said to be the Georgian doorway, intact but impossible for us to see as it faces the river. In 1963 the house was sold to the Apostolic delegate, which attained the status of a diplomatic mission in 1969. Today the home is known as the Apostolic Nunciature.

The only view of it today is through the arched entryway of its picturesque gatehouse. To the left are gracious gardens – vestiges of the old orchard that once flourished here.

Continue down Manor. Just before Coltrin is the start of a private driveway, sweeping off to your left, which leads to the Swedish ambassador's residence. Unfortunately, the house is barely visible from the road. Nonetheless this is another design by Allan Keefer, built for his brother, Thomas.

Now turn left and walk along Coltrin – named after Thomas Coltrin Keefer. To your left is Coltrin Place, a little residential enclave.

On the north corner of Springfield at Coltrin, is the rear of Allan Keefer's last design for Rockcliffe Village, **725 Acacia Avenue, Waterstone**. This is the house he built in 1930 for Frederick E. Bronson. Continue along to Acacia and turn left (north) for just a few paces to appreciate the front of this splendid stone home. Above the carriageway sparkles the gold-coloured stylized chrysanthemum identifying Waterstone as the present residence of the ambassador of Japan. True to period style houses, site orientation was of critical importance. Here, as in many of his designs, Keefer scaled the residence to suit the large lot size.

Retrace your steps on Coltrin to Springfield Road and turn left (south). Walk past the intersection with Thorold. At the southeast corner note the rear of **585 Thorold**, Ambassador of India's residence. The spacious garden sets the mood for this gracious grey stucco house.

Continue south on Springfield. The next rear view is of the back garden of **541 Acacia, Stornoway**, residence of the Leader of the Opposition. This plain stucco structure is by Allan Keefer, built in 1913 for first owner Asconi Joseph Major, who purchased the property for $12,000 from Charles Keefer. In 1923, Ethel Perley-Robertson purchased the house and named it Stornoway after her ancestral home on the Isle of Lewis, Scotland. She hired Allan Keefer to make renovations, adding a bathroom, three bedrooms above the kitchen to accommodate staff, and living quarters above the original stable, today's garage.

During World War II, the Netherlands' Crown Princess Juliana and her children were forced to flee the advancing German army. They escaped in an armoured truck from the Hague and made a hazardous journey to England and then on to Canada. They stayed at Rideau Hall prior to renting 120 Lansdowne (seen later during this walk) and then moved to Stornoway in 1942, where they stayed for the duration of the war.

In March 1950 a private trust was set up by Liberal and Conservative senators to establish a residence for the Leader of the Opposition. In 1970, the government bought Stornoway from the trust for one dollar and turned responsibility for its upkeep to the Department of Public Works. The NCC tends the gardens. Maureen McTeer, who has lived at both Stornoway and 24 Sussex Drive, describes DPW's takeover of Stornoway as unfortunate. Among other renovations, the department, McTeer says, is responsible for the removal of Allan Keefer's trademark *porte-cochère* at the north end of the house in 1978.

Now turn left (east) on Hillcrest and then left again (north) on Acacia. At Crescent, turn right to curve southeast around this street built specifically for brothers Wilson and Harry Southam, founders of the Southam newspaper empire, who both built homes on this street.

Number **11 Crescent, Lindenelm**, the Spanish ambassador's residence, was designed in 1911 by Allan Keefer in a Tudor Revival style for Wilson Mills Southam. The house features a brick ground floor and stuccoed, half-timbered second storey. Note the original slate roof of the house and its numerous gables and dormers.

Frederick Todd, the well-known landscape architect and author of the Ottawa Improvement Commission's 1903 Master Plan for the capital, designed the gardens and recommended the positioning of the house upon its site, overlooking the Ottawa River from the craggy bluffs. Because Lindenelm was designed by both Todd and Keefer, it deserves its special designation under the Ontario Heritage Act.

Number **9 Crescent, Casa Loma**, the Austrian ambassador's residence, was Keefer's 1913 design for Harry Southam. A 1940 fire devastated the original home, but architect A. J. Hazelgrove redesigned Casa Loma, staying true to Keefer's plan. Built in the Elizabethan style the house features a slate roof, and parapet gables that stand clear from the steeply pitched roof. Keefer cleverly designed the Southam brothers' houses to maximize their views over the cliffs to the Ottawa River. As well, their angled frontage onto Crescent Road takes full advantage of the curving street, once their exclusive driveway.

Adjoining number 9 Crescent is **8 Crescent**, the former Admiral Kingsmill House. This was once the residence of Lady Kingsmill, whom the Lord's Day Alliance of Toronto once tried to have arrested for selling coffee on the Sabbath to Suicide Hill ski-jump spectators.

For a completely different architectural flavour, look at **7 Crescent**, the William Teron House. Teron was a major developer of the Ottawa area, perhaps best known for his design of the suburban community of "old" Kanata. There, Teron experimented with an organic approach to house design. His Kanata creations are a combination of cedar, brick, horizontal planes and split levels that take great advantage of natural light and aspect. Number 7 Crescent, built as his own

*7 Crescent nestled into its wooded gardens. Jan. 1992. E. Fletcher*

house in 1970, is designed as three contiguous hexagonals clad in cedar, nestled into pines which screen the view from the street.

Continue along the curving sweep of Crescent. While walking note that the houses on the inside of the street are more modern – and modest – than those overlooking the Ottawa River.

Number **3 Crescent**, the New Zealand ambassador's residence, exhibits the symmetry of a Georgian Colonial Revival house. Regularly spaced windows and dormers and raised side-gables with flanking chimneys give a rhythmical, predictable look to this façade. Note how the brick pilasters create the impression of the centre pavilion characteristic of the Georgian style. Unfortunately, the proportion of this home is set askew by the unwieldy addition at the front with its flat-topped roof with balustrading. Also, there is a clumsy box-like addition on the left which fails to provide a satisfactory balance to the more graceful sitting room extension on the right.

Turn left (east) to descend on Buena Vista, so named because of the beautiful view of MacKay Lake that it gives passersby. Buena Vista is one of several streets with a Spanish name (another is Mariposa: "butterfly") that is another legacy of Rockcliffe developer T. C. Keefer, who visited Mexico at the turn of the century.

Pass 459 Buena Vista on your left (north) and watch for the staircase descending to Cloverdale. Take the stairs and then bear left

*3 Crescent's classical colonial appeal. Jan. 1992. E. Fletcher*

across Cloverdale and walk down Lakehurst to Lansdowne Road South.

In front of you is **412 Lansdowne, Byng House**, the Israeli ambassador's residence. J. W. Ames of Boston – the architect who redesigned Rockcliffe Manor House for Senator Cairine Wilson – designed this house in the style of a French country manor for Colonel H. Willis-O'Connor, who was aide-de-camp and friend to many governors general: Byng, Willingdon, Bessborough, Tweedsmuir, and Athlone. The turret with staggered vertical windows gives the house its special charm. Inside, the turret accommodates a staircase. Of note are the vertical bars masking the windows and doors, a disfiguring security precaution that detracts from the home's otherwise cozy ambiance.

Turn left (north) on Lansdowne. On your left are the two tennis courts that were once the private domain of the Southam brothers. When they were built in 1926 the only house on Lansdowne was **456, Miss Wright's House**. A red brick single family residence, it is similar to houses in the Glebe. This unostentatious home has cut-out maple leaves on the shutters. The shingled third storey is set within the steeply gabled roof, which features dormer windows at either side. This house has a splendid view of the lake.

Next door is **494 Lansdowne**, the Swiss ambassador's residence, which also hugs the lakefront. Built in 1927 by the Kemp-Edwards

*412 Lansdowne. Jan. 1992.* E. Fletcher

family of lumbering renown, the house underwent alterations in 1948 designed by architect W. E. Noffke.

Lansdowne South ends at Hillsdale. Straight ahead of you are the parklands maintained by the NCC. Cross Hillsdale and enter the grassy area. Head to your right and descend the gentle slope to the small stone bridge on Hillsdale over the outflow of MacKay Lake. To the east of this watercourse were the grounds of the Dominion Rifle Range. These then became the National Park accessed by the extension of the Ottawa Electric Railway, which transported Ottawans to the Rockeries opposite Waterstone.

If you followed MacKay Lake's watercourse down to the Ottawa River, you would arrive at the old site of Julius Caesar Blasdell's 1849 steam-driven sawmill, the first in the area. But for today's walk, re-cross Hillsdale and enter the village conservation zone encircling MacKay Lake. To do this, walk through the metal gateway and down the trail following the north side of the lake.

In fall or early spring, when the trees are not in full leaf, there are clear views of the lake's northern bank. Watch for the sudden sighting of a great blue heron, or listen for the rustling skirmish of a chipmunk among autumn's leaves. This is a lakeside worth preserving for its tranquil beauty and what little is left of its natural habitat.

As you walk beside the lake, you see the many additions to the lakeshore built in the late 1980s. Number **700 Hillsdale**, to your left, is architect Wolfgang Mohaupt's modern montage of cedar and stone, at once both angular and sprawling on top of the sloping bank. Next find **710 Hillsdale**, Barry Hobin's traditional English country house of cut stone. Nestled on the edge of the bird sanctuary, its splendid view is somewhat cut off by number 700's later construction. Even in Rockcliffe, "infill" can be irritating.

Keep the lake on your right, following the trail as it winds through the woods. Find and cross a built-up walkway: on your left is the Pond, on your right, MacKay Lake. Note the terraced condominium complex, first of Leonard Koffman's 1986–87 **MacKay Lake Estates** and then, on the right, Barry Hobin's 1988–89 **Bittern Court**, whose staggered brick façade cascades down the steep east bank of the Pond. Their high density population imposes pressures on the wetlands habitat of the park.

Just east of this development and farther behind MacKay Lake is the area marked "Extensive deposit of White Marl" on T. C. Keefer's 1864 map. Thomas Clark operated a brickworks here that supplied both red and white bricks to the entire region. His Rockcliffe white marl brick was popular: the 1877 town hall at Luskville, west of Aylmer in Western Quebec, features corner quoins from here. The Pond itself was not shown on Keefer's map, as it did not exist until 1908, when sand from the site was excavated for construction of the Chateau Laurier. Water flowed in – and the Pond was created.

A branch in the path will take you rather steeply up the southwest embankment of the Pond. You emerge onto Bittern Court. Turn left and walk through the condominium development of Bittern Court that you viewed below. Turn right onto Whitemarl and right again onto Hemlock.

Hemlock is the northeastern boundary of the famous **Beechwood Cemetery**, burial ground of many well-known Rockcliffe and Ottawa residents. Established in 1873, it now has more than 60,000 graves. Here you will find the graves of the MacKays, Keefers, and the poets Archibald Lampman and Duncan Campbell Scott, who are buried adjacent to each other, befitting their close friendship. Exploring the Beechwood cemetery would be a separate walk, and so is not included here.

Continue walking west on Hemlock until you come to the first street, Lansdowne South. On the corner find the grounds of **120 Lansdowne**, "**Noot gedacht**," the residence of the deputy high commissioner of the United Kingdom. This home was originally built in 1938 by John Roper for Col. Shirley E. Woods, historian and inventor of the down-filled vest. Woods rented the premises between 1940 and 1942 to Crown Princess Juliana, before she moved with her family to Stornoway (because 120 was too small). She called the house "Noot gedacht" (Dutch for never thought) because she had never thought that she would have to flee her homeland.[20]

Turn right on Lansdowne and walk along to **115 Lansdowne**, the former **Diefenbaker residence**, on your left. This 1949 house is an unassuming clapboard, colonial-style home, quite without the dominating presence of many Rockcliffe houses. It is the only house that the Diefenbakers ever owned.

Number **187 Lansdowne**, the residence of the ambassador of Iraq, is notable for its imposing security features. A cedar hedge scarcely hides a sturdy steel and concrete fence. Cameras peer down at walkers peering up. Its fortress qualities are emphasized by its situation on the rise of land overlooking MacKay Lake. From this height it commands enviable views of the lake and pond.

Continue down Lansdowne until you reach the sharp turn to the left, at Mariposa. Here, veer to your right instead and then turn immediately left, along the path known as the Dog Walk that leads quietly behind Sylvan Way.

Number **250 Sylvan, the Ledges,** is the second house on the path, and was built in 1934 by architect A. J. Hazelgrove for well-known Ottawa businessman Lawrence Freiman. Its layered planes and hipped roof are particularly well suited to the terraced slopes. A later sunroom addition with cantilevered corner arches adds interest to the original structure.

Next door, the third house, is **245 Sylvan**, the **Rowley Home**, was built for Graham Rowley, eminent Arctic explorer and geologist. Its 1909 date makes it an early home in Rockcliffe Village. Rowley would have looked down on both MacKay Lake and the Southam's twin tennis courts. Rounded fieldstones from the excavation were used in its façade. From this lakeside perspective, the heavy-looking black roof appears gambrel-shaped: however, if seen from its front façade on Sylvan, it shows a mansard style roof. These features, along with its stuccoed, round-cornered tower, give it an eclectic look.

The path ends at the corner of Prospect. Stop to look at **400 Lansdowne**, the **Hart Massey House**. This design won the coveted Massey medal in 1959 and is important for several reasons. First because of its modernist, avant-garde design. Turning their backs on vernacular and revivalist designs, which looked to the past for inspiration, modernists experimented with new structural technologies. They stripped buildings of unnecessary accoutrements. The result was an entire movement inspired by the Bauhaus and International Style groups in Europe.

Here architect Hart Massey experimented with basic rectangles, or cubes, projecting from the hillside. The house's steel supports are entirely visible, being painted black for emphasis. They echo the verticals of the surrounding tree trunks – an effect which is dramatically enhanced by a fresh winter snowfall. The steel supports have another intriguing design feature: within the modular steel frame, the cubes were designed so that they could be added to or interchanged.

Now climb up Prospect, with the lake at your back. Cross Cloverdale and immediately watch out for the steps leading up the hillside to Fernbank.

Note **393 Fernbank,** on your right as you emerge from the steps onto the street. This is an English country "cottage," built between

*400 Lansdowne, Hart Massey's "cubist creation." The accented steel supports mimic the vertical lines of the surrounding trees. Jan. 1992. E. Fletcher*

the wars and designed by W. E. Noffke after the fashion of English architects Edwin Lutyens and C. F. A. Voysey. Both were popular architects in the Arts and Crafts Movement. The steep asymmetrical main gable with its flaring buttresses is mirrored by a smaller gable housing a sunroom to the right of the main arched doorway. Two flanking chimneys with sloped offsets further balance the house. The design is charming, situated as it is atop the hill overlooking MacKay Lake.

Continue on Fernbank to Acacia. Cross Acacia and note the width of this street. It is one of the main arteries of Rockcliffe Village, with houses set well back from the road. After a few paces to your right, turn left (west) on Buchan. Number **270 Buchan** is another colonial house with a pronounced horizontal composition. Its first storey is limestone, the second is clapboard and the third horizontal layer is its steeply pitched roof with dormers. Shutters accentuate the house's New England colonial look.

At the corner of Buchan and Mariposa, you can see the grounds of **Ashbury College**. Cross Mariposa and walk a few paces east (left). The main building was designed by Allan Keefer in a utilitarian red brick Elizabethan period style. Keefer had attended Ashbury in 1891 at its former location on Argyle Avenue, the present site of the Windsor Arms apartments, opposite the Canadian Museum of Nature. The new site in Rockcliffe was purchased from the Rockcliffe Property Company for $12,000. In 1910 the school opened at its new location.

The grounds of the school were once a rocky field. It was cleared by Ashbury's handyman, Fred Oliver, who built the rock walls surrounding the school from the fieldstone. It was Oliver who dug, lifted and hauled every stone to its place along Springfield, Mariposa and Glenwood.

Turn west (right) to cross Mariposa, and then cross diagonally through the **Jubilee Garden**, the centre of the village. As you approach Springfield Road, you walk through the **Village Green**. This central park was planned under the direction of Humphrey Carver as a community Canadian Centennial project in 1967. Rockcliffe residents planted trees and erected lampposts to create a "people place" out of a former tangle of rocks and bush.

You are now on Springfield. Turn right to walk beside **Rockcliffe Public School** and the **Police Station**. Princess Juliana's children attended this school during the war years when the family resided in Rockcliffe. The Princess chose to send her children to a public rather than a private school, and so her children enjoyed a regular rather than an exclusively privileged and protected life while in Rockcliffe. On April 22, 1952, as Queen Juliana, she returned to Rockcliffe to lay the cornerstone of the gymnasium and community hall at the public school. The stone is still visible although somewhat overgrown. As a gift of thanks to Canada for providing her family a refuge in wartime, she donated thousands of tulip bulbs that were used to grace the parkland around Dow's Lake and the Queen Elizabeth Driveway.

Now turn left on Buena Vista and proceed north. On your right is the third village school, **261 Buena Vista, Elmwood**. Situated on the former MacKay farm of the same name, the old rambling farmhouse was occupied for years by Charles Keefer, son of T. C. and father of architect Allan. The school's playing fields preserve the lovely openness at the heart of Rockcliffe.

Elmwood was founded by the wife of one of Ashbury College's teachers, Mrs. Hamlet S. Philpott, in 1915 as the Rockcliffe Preparatory School serving both boys and girls. In 1923 it became a private

*Elmwood's half-timbered façade and red roof add colour to Buena Vista. Jan. 1992.*
E. Fletcher

girls' school. That year saw the addition of a dormitory wing and an assembly hall. In 1925 the original stone farmhouse was demolished.

Turn right on Manor Avenue and cross to the far side of the street. Watch carefully for David Thomas Laneway leading off to the left (if you reach Hillcrest you've gone too far). Walk down the narrow lane and emerge onto Minto Place. Turn right on Minto Place and go a few steps until you reach Soper Place. Pause and look to your left.

The pocket of land described by Soper Place used to be the site of Thomas MacKay's stone Victorian Gothic "cottage," Birkenfels. The story of this last part of the original MacKay Estate is a sad reflection of Rockcliffe's infill and density pressures. Birkenfels property owners Mike and Tim Perley-Robertson obtained permission from Rockcliffe Village to subdivide this once fine old house with its estate grounds into eighteen lots. Rumour has it that the estate was divided such that the limestone house straddled *two* lots, and was thus far too expensive to purchase and restore. Birkenfels, Rockcliffe's oldest house, was torn down in the summer of 1991, despite the outcry of heritage-minded village residents. Loss of the historic building is inestimable. Because the house is gone and the estate divided, the name Birkenfels now has no meaning.

In March of 1993, only three lots have houses. Immediately to your left is **272 Soper Place**, an immense home erected in 1992–93. Its

Georgian details include the symmetrical arrangement of windows and an imposing central doorway pavilion. Brilliant white corner quoins are sharply at odds with the red brick façade. This oversized house dominates its lot, achieving a startlingly ungainly effect at the entrance to Birkenfels grounds.

On the right, notice the twin gables of the original Birkenfels carriage house and stables, now **299 Soper Place**, transformed in 1992 by architect Richard Limmert into a spectacular collage of forms and materials for businessman Michael Potter. A limestone wall extension to the northwest of the home cleverly shields the gardens from public scrutiny. It also masks the rear glassed extension of the home, which accommodates a sunken living room with a cozy fireplace. The original Birkenfels house stood on the far side of the wall. To the east at the rear is a separate building housing a swimming pool, connected to the main house by an outside walkway.

Beyond these transformed Birkenfels stables find another Barry Hobin creation, **247 Soper Place** completed in 1991. It also possesses design elements reminiscent of both Wright and Noffke as evidenced most particularly in its window treatment, horizontal composition and mix of sheer stucco with rough-cut stone walls.

Now turn around and walk back to MacKinnon. Turn right. On the corner is **95 MacKinnon**, once home to Thomas Coltrin Keefer

*247 Soper Place. Jan. 1993.* K. Fletcher

and his wife, Annie [MacKay] MacKinnon. This picturesque clap-board cottage and its garden are lovingly maintained. The house features a steep gable with dentil trim and peaked window mould-ings, both common details of Victorian vernacular cottages.

By 1903 the couple had moved to the Manor House, and Keefer sold the summer cottage to William Gerard, a former New Edinburgh resident. Gerard was millwright and superintendent with the Maclaren mills in New Edinburgh. He brought his wife and nine children to this little cottage (*see* New Edinburgh walk).

As you walk down MacKinnon, you will see Gerard's legacy to Rockcliffe. In 1912, after his wife died, he built 79 MacKinnon, and in successive years built two other homes both for his sons: in 1915 number 63 and, in 1923, number 49. They lack the grandeur and prominent situations of many of the houses in Rockcliffe. Like the red brick house you saw earlier at 456 Lansdowne, these houses on MacKinnon are similar to houses in the Glebe neighbourhood.

MacKinnon ends abruptly, joining Birkenfels Road. Turn left here and then almost immediately right onto Buena Vista, which in turn ends at Lisgar. At the corner is **412 Lisgar**. There is no unifying focal point to this home, which sprawls over its sloping site in a confusing collection of competing textures.

*420 Lisgar, the organic lines of the Danish Embassy help it blend into its hillside location. Jan. 1992. E. Fletcher*

Compare 412 with the organic design of **420 Lisgar**, the Danish ambassador's residence. While the former imposes itself upon passersby, number 420 is a masterpiece of environmental integration. It is neatly tucked into the slope. Its cedar grillwork averts the fortress-like aspect of the ground-floor concrete retaining wall. The cedar staining of the vertical woodwork of the main and second floors fronting Lisgar is set off by vermilion window trim. Its horizontal planes and successful integration into the hillside may seem to be strongly evocative of Frank Lloyd Wright's style. However, post-and-beam construction with broad eaves is also common to Scandinavian architecture.

Complete this walk of Rockcliffe by ambling through the gentle wooded slopes of the park, first heading to your right on Lisgar and then continuing on the Rockcliffe Parkway to return to your car at the Lookout. If you parked at the bandshell, cross the Rockcliffe Parkway and walk through the Pine Knoll down to the parking lot.

# Glossary

**Arcade**: an arched passageway, usually along a wall.

**Ashlar**: rough-cut stone "bricks".

**Atrium**: an enclosed well within a multi-storey building, often now roofed with glass.

**Bargeboard**: decorative boards along edge of gable or roof, also called gingerbread.

**Board and batten**: a vertical cladding of planks with protective trim nailed over the joints.

**Boss**: a raised ornament or knob.

**Buttress**: integral wall supports, built at right angles to the wall.

**Capitals**: the very top of a column or pillar, often decorated.

**Chamfer**: a bevel or groove.

**Cinquefoil**: clover-like design with five "leaves."

**Clapboard**: a cladding of horizontal overlapping planks.

**Colonnette**: a small, non-structural column.

**Coping**: the sloped top of a wall.

**Corbel**: a stone or timber projecting from a wall to support a weight or for decoration.

**Corinthian**: a style of column with ornate capitals.

**Cornice**: the projecting moulding at the top of a building or wall.

**Crenellation**: the classic castle wall-top with alternating spaces and walls, also called a battlement.

**Crocket**: ornament, usually shaped as foliage, that projects from a pinnacle, gable, spire, etc.

**Cupola**: a small round dome atop a roof.

**Curtain wall**: exterior non-load-bearing wall.

**Dentil trim**: small, tooth-like decorative moulding, usually under a cornice.

**Doric**: a style of column with plain capitals.

**Dormer**: a projecting window in a sloping roof.

**Entablature**: the horizontal beam that spans two or more columns.

**Façade**: the front wall of any building, or the faces of several buildings along a street.

**Fenestration**: the arrangement of windows in any building.

**Finial**: the topmost ornament on gable, pediment, etc.

**Flashing**: metal strip over a roof joint that prevents water seepage.

**Gable**: triangular upper part of a wall under a ridged roof.

**Gambrel**: a roof consisting of a lower steeply sloping part and an upper, ridged and gabled part.

**Gargoyle**: carved grotesque in the form of a water spout projecting from the gutter.

**Gingerbread**: *see* Bargeboard.

**Grotesque**: fanciful ornament, usually a caricature of an animal or human.

**Hipped roof**: one that slopes from a central ridge on the ends as well as the sides.

**Ionic**: a style of column with a capital of two ornamental scrolls.

**Lancet window**: narrow window with pointed head.

**Lintel**: horizontal timber or stone over doorway or window opening.

**Mansard**: a roof with two slopes on each side, the upper almost flat, and the lower slope very steep and usually pierced with dormers.

**Mouldings**: material such as stone or brick used as a surround, or trim, framing a window or door.

**Mullion**: a vertical bar dividing a window.

**Oriel window**: a bay window that projects from an upper storey and is supported by corbels.

**Palladian**: neoclassical style characterized by a central arch flanked by rectangular openings.

**Parapet**: a low wall or railing around a roof.

**Pediment**: triangular section above an opening, especially above the portico in classical Greek buildings.

**Pier**: the upright, solid wall between windows, pillars supporting an arch or projecting canopy over an entryway.

**Pilaster**: an ornamental, non-load-bearing pillar.

**Pinnacle**: small, ornamental turret or tower.

*Porte-cochère*: a covered entry extending over the width of a path or driveway.

**Portico**: a porch fashioned as a roof supported by columns.

**Quatrefoil**: clover-like design with four "leaves."

**Quoin**: stones or bricks, often decorative, forming the corner of a building.

**Rustication**: deep-set masonry joins, sometimes used to exaggerate the base of ground-floor walls.

**Sill**: horizontal timber or stone that foots a door or window opening.

**Skeleton frame construction**: a freestanding, load-bearing frame of iron or of steel upon which are hung floors and exterior and interior walls.

**Spandrel**: structural horizontal sections of a wall between windows and vertical piers, or the section of a wall described inside a pediment or arch.

**Stringcourse**: a raised horizontal band of bricks or stones.

**Terracotta**: fired, unglazed red pottery.

**Tracery**: decorative stone or woodwork separating the glass at the head of a window.

**Transom**: a horizontal bar dividing a window, or horizontal window above a door or another window.

**Trefoil**: clover-like design with three "leaves."

**Voussoir**: the wedge-shaped stones that form an arch.

# Endnotes

1. Bourinot, Arthur, editor "Letter to Dr. Pelham Edgar, Feb. 11, 1916" *More Letters of Duncan Campbell Scott*, Rockcliffe Park, 1960, p. 8.

2. Lett, William P., *The City of Ottawa and Its Surroundings*, A. S. Woodburn Press, Ottawa, 1884, p. 5.

3. MacTaggart, John, *Three Years in Canada*, Volume 1, page 162, 1829.

4. John By to the Ordnance Board in letter dated January 19, 1829, as found in Michael Newton's *Lower Town Ottawa, 1826–54*, Volume 1, Manuscript Report 104, p. 76.

5. Gwyn, Sandra, *The Private Capital*, McClelland & Stewart, 1984, p. 202.

6. Abbott, George F., *Abbott's Guide to Ottawa, Hull & Vicinity*, 2nd Edition, Ottawa, 1911, p. 11.

7. *The Journal*, August 13, 1888, letter to the editor entitled "Speaking Out."

8. *The Ottawa Packet and Weekly Commercial Gazette*, Dec. 22, 1849.

9. Fréchette, Annie Howells, "Life at Rideau Hall," *Harper's New Monthly Magazine*. July 1881. Volume LXII, No. CCCLXXIV.

10. Gwyn, Sandra, *The Private Capital*. p. 209.

11. Askwith, John. *Recollections of New Edinburgh*, 1923 [no page numbers]

12. *The Ottawa Citizen.*, 21 February, 1875.

13. *The Ottawa Citizen.*, July 14, 1992.

14. Ricketts, Shannon, *W. E. Noffke, An Ottawa Architect*, City of Ottawa, 1990. p. 67.

15. Desbarats, Lilian Scott, *Recollections*, p. 48, Ottawa, 1957.

16. Meredith, Colbourne, "Short Talk Before the Woman's Canadian Historical Society of Ottawa." PAC–MG29E62 Vol. 8. p. 6.

17. Meredith, Colbourne, "My Victorian 80s and 90s," unpublished manuscript, MG29E62 Vol. 10.

18. Gwyn, Sandra, *The Private Capital*, p. 238.

19. Walker, H & O., *The Carleton Saga*, p. 313.

20. Kalman, H. & Roaf, J., *Exploring Ottawa*, University of Toronto Press, 1983. p. 135.

Note re photo credits: NAC refers to the National Archives of Canada; PAC refers to the Public Archives of Canada (now renamed the NAC); and NCC refers to the National Capital Commission.

Note re spelling: although both are commonly used, throughout the text I have used Thomas "MacKay" not "McKay".

# Further Reading

The following books represent only a few of the resources that have been indispensable aids to my understanding and appreciation of the history and architecture of the capital. I recommend all of these books to you for your further reading enjoyment.

Note that the list does not include archival resources. I encourage interested readers to go to the National Archives on Wellington to peruse the manuscript, photographic and architectural and mapping collections. Also, the City of Ottawa Archives with its helpful staff, books, photographs, computer records and city bylaws, located on Stanley Street, New Edinburgh, is a rich mine of information. Neighbourhood community associations, Heritage Ottawa and the archives of *The Ottawa Citizen* – as well as many journalists there, are equally fine sources of information. In particular, the National Capital Commission Library and the Ottawa Room of the Metcalfe public library offers many rare manuscripts of the city. As well, many newspapers and periodicals were of value.

Lastly, of special note were newspaper correspondents such as "Amaryllis" and Annie Howells Fréchette in the late 1800s, and the more contemporary Gladys Blair and Madge MacBeth, who wrote lively columns for a variety of publications.

Askwith, John E., "Recollections of New Edinburgh", *Burgh Breeze Bits*, 1923.

Bernstein, William, and Cawker, Ruth. *Contemporary Canadian Architecture*, Fitzhenry & Whiteside, 1988.

Blumenson, John, *Ontario Architecture A Guide to Styles and Terms*, Fitzhenry & Whiteside, 1990.

Bond, C. C. J., *City on the Ottawa*; Queen's Printer, 1971.

Brault, Lucien, *The Mile of History*, National Capital Commission.

———, *Ottawa Old & New*, Ottawa Historical Information Institute, 1946.

Carver, H., *The Cultural Landscape of Rockcliffe Park Village*, Village of Rockcliffe Park, 1985.

Desbarats, Lilian Scott, *Recollections*, Ottawa, 1957.

Eggleston, Wilfrid, *The Queen's Choice*, National Capital Commission, Ottawa, 1961.

Farr, David, *A Church in the Glebe: St Matthew's Anglican Church, Ottawa, 1898–1988.*

Gard, Anson A., *The Hub and the Spokes*, Emerson Press, 1904.

German, Tony, *A Character of its Own: Ashbury College 1891–1991*, Creative Bound, 1991.

Guernsay, Terry G., *Statues of Parliament Hill: An Illustrated History*, National Capital Commission, 1986.

Gwyn, Sandra, *The Private Capital*, McClelland & Stewart, 1984.

Kalman, Harold and Roaf, John, *Exploring Ottawa, An Architectural Guide to the Nation's Capital*, University of Toronto Press, 1983.

Leaning, John and Fortin, Lyette, *Our Architectural Ancestry*, Haig & Haig.

Leggett, Robert, *Rideau Waterway*, University of Toronto Press, 1972.

Lett, William Pitman, *Recollections of Bytown and Its Old Inhabitants*, Citizen Printing and Publishing Co., Ottawa, 1874.

McTeer, Maureen, *Residences – Homes of Canada's Leaders*, Prentice-Hall Inc. 1982.

Maitland, Leslie and Taylor, Louis, *Historical Sketches of Ottawa*, Broadview Press, 1990.

Maitland, Leslie, Hucker, Jacqueline & Ricketts, Shannon, *A Guide to Canadian Architectural Styles*, Broadview Press, 1992.

Mika, Nick and Helma, *Bytown: The Early Days of Ottawa*, Mika Publishing Co., 1982.

Newton, Michael, *Lower Town Ottawa, Volume 1: 1826–1854*, Manuscript Report 104, NCC 1979.

Newton, Michael, *Lower Town Ottawa, Volume 2: 1854–1900*, Manuscript Report 106, NCC 1981.

Phillips, R. A. J., *The East Block of the Parliament Buildings of Canada*, Ottawa, 1967.

Ricketts, Shannon, *W.E. Noffke: An Ottawa Architect*, City of Ottawa, 1990.

Rybczynski, Witold, *Home*, Penguin Books, 1986.

Smith, Julian, et al. *Byward Market Heritage Conservation District Study*, 1990.

Taylor, C. J., *Some Early Ottawa Buildings*, Historical Research Section, Canadian Inventory of Historic Buildings, 1975.

Taylor, John H., *Ottawa, An Illustrated History*, James Lorimer & Co., 1986.

Walker, Harry, and Walker, Olive, *The Carleton Saga*, Runge Press, 1968.

# Acknowledgements

A mine of heritage information and a warm human being died in 1991. Michael Newton, former chief historian of the National Capital Commission was with me in spirit, however, as I perused his historical files at the NCC and walked my walks. *Capital Walks* is indebted to his scrupulous attention to detail as documented in his files and notes.

Several NCC staff members gave me expert advice and access to photographic and other historical records. Among them are Denis Drever, chief photographer, and his 1992 summer assistant, Paddye Thomas. Denis gave me free access to the NCC photographic files; Paddye reproduced many of the NCC heritage photographs used in these pages. Lark Hodgins, chief of systems and practices, information holdings; Gwyneth Hughes, head of library services; and Nancy Veenstra, supervisor of central records operations cheerfully granted special access to Michael Newton's heritage files and somehow managed to answer all of my many queries.

Brian Meredith granted me permission to quote from his father's, architect Colbourne (Coly) Meredith's, unpublished memoirs.

Bruce Weedmark, architectural archivist, of the National Archives, Cartographic and Audio-visual Architectural Archives Division tirelessly answered detailed questions.

Louise Roy-Brochu, chief archivist at the City of Ottawa Archives and City archivists David Bullock and Serge Barbe paid similar attention to details. Particular thanks go to Serge, who scrupulously read my manuscript for historical accuracy.

Architectural designer and illustrator Michael Neelin also read the manuscript and walked the eight walks, checked the maps and, most importantly, acted as my architectural research assistant, ensuring my terms and points of reference were appropriate. Architect Barry Hobin kindly responded to my last-minute requests for specific details of many buildings.

By-Rideau Councillor Richard Cannings provided his special heritage perspective, list of contacts and personal encouragement to my project.

Masonry stove builder Norbert Senf provided details about masonry construction and engineering. Both he and Leila Nulty-Senf offered cheerful, unflagging support of *Capital Walks* from its inception.

Dinah Forbes at McClelland & Stewart is that rare breed of editor who dispenses excellent advice in a discerning, sensitive manner.

Thanks to Eric Fletcher, who walked every walk with me, produced all the maps, and helped me execute the final design and layout of *Capital Walks* on our Macintosh computer.

Finally, thanks to my mother and father, who nurtured in me a lifelong respect and appreciation of the arts, architecture and the outdoors.

Thank you, one and all.

# Index

The index includes architects, important historical figures and also the names and street addresses of buildings found in Capital Walks. Numerals in bold indicate page numbers of photographs.